AMERICA the BEAUTIFUL

UTAH

By Betty McCarthy

Consultants

John E. Ord, Ed.D., Social Studies Specialist; Professor of Education, Brigham Young University; author of *Utah History Program*

John S. McCormick, Ph.D., Professor of History, Social Science Department, Salt Lake Community College; former Historian, Utah State Historical Society

David L. Walton, Ph.D., Media Coordinator and former Master Teacher Utah History Consultant, Alpine School District, American Fork; contributing author to Ord and Stone, *Individualized Utah History Curriculum*

Robert L. Hillerich, Ph.D., Bowling Green State University, Bowling Green, Ohio

CHILDRENS PRESS®
CHICAGO

A sandstone arch in Zion National Park

Project Editor: Joan Downing
Associate Editor: Shari Joffe
Design Director: Margrit Fiddle
Typesetting: Graphic Connections, Inc.
Engraving: Liberty Photoengraving

Library of Congress Cataloging-in-Publication Data

McCarthy, Betty.
   America the beautiful. Utah / by Betty McCarthy.
      p.   cm.
   Includes index.
   Summary: Introduces the geography, history,
government, economy, industry, culture, historic
sites, and famous people of this Western state.
      ISBN 0-516-00490-5
   1. Utah—Juvenile literature.   2. Utah.
I.   Title.
F826.3.M3   1989   89-35083
979.2—dc20   CIP
                                          AC

The Mormon Assembly Hall and the *Sea Gull* monument in Temple Square, Salt Lake City

TABLE OF CONTENTS

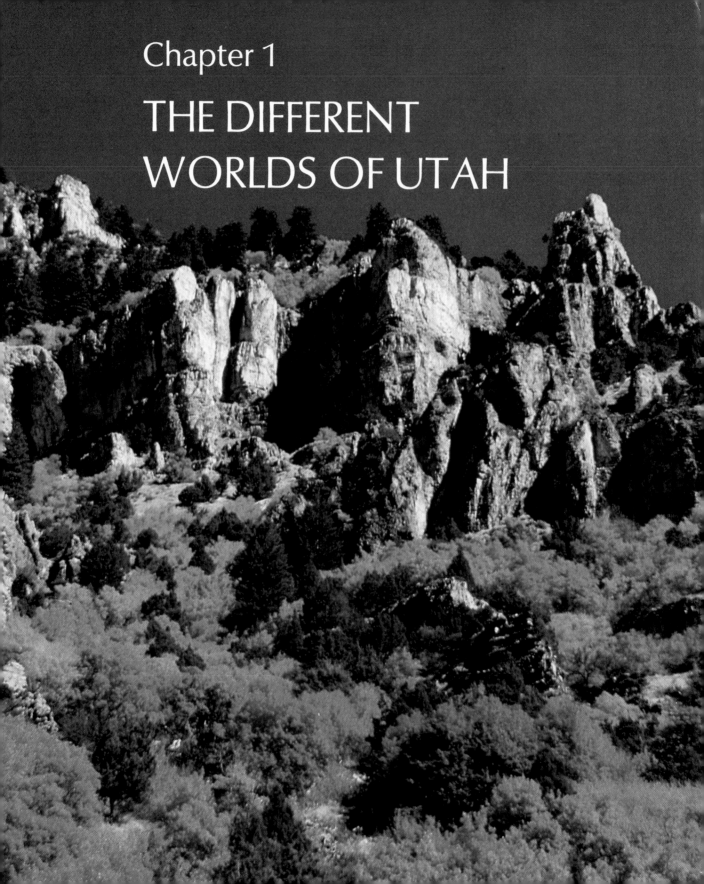

Chapter 1

THE DIFFERENT WORLDS OF UTAH

THE DIFFERENT WORLDS OF UTAH

Ask any ten people, even ten Utahans, what Utah is really like, and you will get ten different answers. Utah is unique. Utah is the only state in the nation dominated by a single contemporary religion. Seven of every ten Utahans are Mormons, members of the Church of Jesus Christ of Latter-day Saints.

Utah's varied landscape has been called the most grand and glorious scenery in the world. Pale greys, violets, pinks, and blues characterize the Great Basin in western Utah. Hot reds, oranges, and golds color the south and east. Cool green and forested mountains dominate north-central Utah.

The federal government set aside some of Utah's most beautiful scenery for national parks. Only Alaska has more national parks than Utah. The state government also set aside land for state parks. Even so, there is so much beauty left over that unclaimed and unnamed treasures lie along every highway and hiking trail.

Of the more than five million visitors to the state each year, about half see only the state's largest cities. They come on a pilgrimage to the Mormon capital of the world at Salt Lake City, on business to bustling commercial centers, or to ski the "greatest snow on earth" in the nearby Wasatch Mountains.

About half of Utah's annual visitors never see a town with a population larger than four thousand. They go directly to Utah's awe-inspiring scenery and its remote wilderness areas.

Which is the real Utah? It depends on whom you ask.

Chapter 2
THE LAND

THE LAND

. . . ascending to the summit, immediately at our feet
[we] beheld the object of our anxious search—the waters
of the Inland Sea, stretching in still and solitary
grandeur far beyond the limit of our vision. . . .
It was one of the great points of the exploration.
—John Charles Frémont, September 6, 1843

GEOGRAPHY AND TOPOGRAPHY

Located in the Rocky Mountains of the western United States,
Utah lies midway between Canada to the north and Mexico to the
south. With a total area of 84,899 square miles (219,888 square
kilometers), Utah is the eleventh-largest state in the nation.

Utah's boundaries are straight lines and right angles, cut across
the map without regard to rivers, mountains, or deserts. The state
is rectangular in shape except for a corner cut out of the northeast.
States that border Utah are Idaho on the north, Wyoming on the
northeast, Colorado on the east, Arizona on the south, and
Nevada on the west. Utah's southeast corner is the only spot in
the United States where four states come together. Utah, Colorado,
New Mexico, and Arizona meet at this "Four Corners" region.

The state has three major land regions: the Basin and Range
Region, the Rocky Mountains, and the Colorado Plateau. The
Basin and Range Region covers the western third of Utah. It is
dry, flat land, broken only by scattered mountain ranges and

The Wasatch Mountains from Mount Nebo, near Nephi

valleys. John Charles Frémont, the famous western explorer, named it the Great Basin when he recognized that it was a completely enclosed depression in the land, with no outlet to the sea. The Great Salt Lake in the northeastern part of the basin is much saltier than any sea except the Dead Sea because many rivers flow into it, but none flow out. When the water evaporates, great salt deposits are left behind. West and southwest of the lake are three extensive deserts—the Great Salt Lake, the Escalante, and the Sevier.

Utah's portion of the Rocky Mountain Region includes the Wasatch and Uinta ranges. The Wasatch Mountains run 150 miles (241 kilometers) north from Mount Nebo, near Nephi, to the Utah-Idaho border. Together with high plateaus farther south, this range forms part of the eastern rim of the Great Basin. Utah's major metropolitan areas—Ogden, Salt Lake City, and Orem-Provo—are nestled along the Wasatch Front between rugged mountains on the east and the Great Basin on the west. A fault line along the same front poses a real danger of severe earthquakes, although the modern era has seen only mild tremors.

Dead Horse Point, in the Island in the Sky district of Canyonlands National Park, overlooks the deep gorge carved over the ages by the Colorado River.

The wild and beautiful Uinta Mountains run east-west along the Utah-Wyoming border from Colorado almost to Salt Lake City. It is the only mountain range in the country that runs in an east-west direction. Twin-domed Kings Peak, at 13,528 feet (4,123 meters) Utah's highest mountain, is part of this range. Ten other peaks in the Uintas soar above 13,000 feet (3,962 meters).

About half of Utah lies in the Colorado Plateau, east and south of the Wasatch-Uinta ranges. Here is some of the state's most magnificent scenery. The Green and Colorado rivers have cut deep and glorious canyons lined with many-hued rock walls. Water and wind have sculpted fantastically shaped rock formations. For centuries, human beings have marveled at the mystic shapes and colors, seeing in them gods and demons, castles and bridges.

RIVERS AND LAKES

Utah measures its 3,000 square miles (7,770 square kilometers) of water very carefully. Each square foot is important in a nearly arid land.

Gateway to the Narrows, in Zion National Park, is a deep, narrow canyon with sheer, steep walls. It was created by the action of the Virgin River.

The Bear, Provo, and Weber rivers arise in the Uinta Mountains, flow westward across the Wasatch Mountains, and drain into the Great Salt Lake. Where they exit the Wasatch, such rivers have deposited large deltas of fertile soil. The first Mormon settlers clustered at these deltas, harnessed the river waters for irrigation, and created rich farmland.

Utah's largest rivers, the Colorado and the Green, drain the eastern half of the state. Flowing south and southwestward, the two rivers and their many tributaries are an important water supply for Utah and its neighboring states.

The Sevier is the main river of south-central Utah. It ends its course in the Great Basin, disappearing before it reaches the usually dry Sevier Lake. The Jordan River flows north from Utah Lake, emptying into the Great Salt Lake. The Virgin River, in the southwest, flows out of the state into Nevada's Lake Mead. In the northwest, the Raft River flows into Idaho's Snake River.

Lake Powell, Utah's largest man-made lake, was formed by a dam on the Colorado River.

The Great Salt Lake is Utah's largest natural lake. It is completely landlocked. The saltiness, depth, and size of the Great Salt Lake depend on evaporation and precipitation. At low levels, it is about eight times saltier than the Pacific Ocean. Though its average depth is only 13 feet (4 meters), it has reached 34 feet (10 meters) in wet years. In 1983, the Great Salt Lake flooded its banks, threatening Salt Lake City some 20 miles (32 kilometers) away. At that time, the lake covered more than 1,700 square miles (4,403 square kilometers), a little more area than the state of Rhode Island.

Utah Lake in north-central Utah and Bear Lake at the Utah-Idaho border are the only other large natural lakes in the state. Both are freshwater lakes. In addition, thousands of small glacial lakes dot Utah's Wasatch and Uinta mountains.

Utah's largest man-made lake is Lake Powell, in the south. Nearly 200 miles (322 kilometers) long, it was formed by a dam on the Colorado River. Flaming Gorge Reservoir, on the Green River in the northeast, is 90 miles (145 kilometers) long. It is shared by Utah and Wyoming. The Upper Colorado River Storage

Project, as well as irrigation projects on every other possible river, have created hundreds of dams and small storage lakes throughout the state.

CLIMATE

Sunny Utah enjoys some three hundred cloudless days each year. It is one of the driest states in the nation, second only to Nevada. Average annual precipitation (rain and snow) varies widely throughout the state, from less than 5 inches (13 centimeters) in the Great Basin and Colorado Plateau regions to almost 50 inches (127 centimeters) in parts of the Wasatch and Uinta mountains. Salt Lake City averages 15 inches (38 centimeters) of precipitation each year.

Throughout Utah, summers are long and warm and winters are short and mild. Temperatures often dip below freezing between November and April. Only rarely, however, do they drop below 0 degrees Fahrenheit (minus 18 degrees Celsius). The state's "hot spot," appropriately called "Dixie," sweltered at 117 degrees Fahrenheit (47 degrees Celsius) on July 5, 1985, when Utah's highest temperature was recorded at St. George. Woodruff, on February 6, 1899, and Strawberry Tunnel, on January 5, 1913, experienced Utah's lowest recorded temperature of minus 50 degrees Fahrenheit (minus 46 degrees Celsius).

Extreme temperature differences sometimes occur within just a few miles. An amazed tourist in Canyonlands National Park recalls broiling under the July sun when temperatures topped 100 degrees Fahrenheit (37.8 degrees Celsius). Having driven less than 50 miles (80 kilometers) up the slope to the nearest high campground for relief, she was awakened in the middle of the night by snow collapsing the roof of her tent!

Among the wildflowers found in Utah are (left to right) sego lilies, shown here in Capitol Reef National Park; Indian paintbrush, pictured in Arches National Park; and lupine and Indian paintbrush making a splash of color in Little Cottonwood Canyon, east of Salt Lake City.

PLANT AND ANIMAL LIFE

The sego lily, Utah's state flower, is found throughout the state. Its bulbous root was a staple in the diet of early Indians and a blessing to many a Mormon pioneer waiting for the crops to come in.

The mountains and highlands are blanketed with seasonal displays of dogtooth violets, sweet William, roses, and many other wildflowers. Indian paintbrush colors the dry canyons and plateaus with its bright orange or red spikes. In the Great Basin, sagebrush was once the dominant wild plant. But where irrigation is possible, it has been cleared to make way for cash crops.

Vast national forests clothe nearly a third of Utah. Trees in the forested Wasatch and Uinta mountains include bristlecone pines, some specimens three thousand years old, fir, aspen, and blue spruce, the state tree. Gnarled junipers and piñon pines grow in the drier plateau and highland areas. At lower elevations, willows and cottonwoods follow the life-giving mountain streams. Pink flowering tamarisk, also called salt cedar, thrives in the washes and streams of the south.

Flocks of sea gulls, the state bird, nest and breed around the shores of the Great Salt Lake.

Buffalo herds live on Antelope Island in the Great Salt Lake, and small herds inhabit the Henry Mountains. Wild mustangs are found in western desert valleys. Mule deer, elk, antelope, moose, sheep, and mountain goats roam the highlands. Black bears, mountain lions, bobcats, coyotes, and other animals often follow the same hunting trails.

Beavers, minks, otters, and foxes flourish now that the fur trappers have gone. Rabbits, small rodents, porcupines, and prairie dogs dart to and from cover in Utah's dry canyons and basins. Snakes, lizards, and desert tortoises pose motionless in the sunbaked sands and rocks.

Utah's lakes and rivers teem with bass, catfish, suckers, carp, perch, and trout. The cutthroat trout is unique to western Utah's Deep Creek Mountains. Fishermen boast of record-making 40-pound (18-kilogram) trout caught at Flaming Gorge Reservoir.

Thousands of migratory waterfowl, including Utah's state bird, the sea gull, nest and breed around the shores of the Great Salt Lake. Eagles, hawks, vultures, and other birds of prey hunt the plateaus. Tiny finches and tuneful meadowlarks are among the many smaller birds that find Utah to their liking.

Chapter 3
THE PEOPLE

THE PEOPLE

Utahans tend to be younger and healthier than the national average. Life expectancy in Utah is well above the national average. Utah's birthrate is the highest in the nation, double the national average. And the number of infant deaths in Utah is lower than the national average.

POPULATION AND POPULATION DISTRIBUTION

With 1,461,037 people, according to the 1980 census, Utah ranked only thirty-sixth among the states in population. Between 1970 and 1980, however, Utah's population grew by an amazing 37.9 percent, more than three times the national average for the same period. Utah's 1986 population was estimated at 1,665,000, an increase of 14 percent since 1980.

Eight of every ten Utahans live in urban areas (cities with populations of 2,500 or more). The state's largest cities are Salt Lake City, Provo, Ogden, and Orem, all along the Wasatch Front. Utah's wild canyonlands and arid wastelands are thinly populated. Population density averages only about 17 people per square mile (7 people per square kilometer) throughout the state. By contrast, little New Jersey averages 940 people per square mile (363 people per square kilometer).

WHO ARE THE UTAHANS?

Most Utahans—about 97 percent—were born in the United States. Most of the remaining 3 percent were born in Canada, Germany, Great Britain, or Mexico.

Native Americans are Utah's largest minority group, numbering just over 19,000 in the 1980 census. Although many live in and near the large cities, tribal reservations are home to about 12,500 people. The largest is the Utes' Uintah and Ouray Reservation and its Hill Creek Extension in eastern and northeastern Utah. The extensive Navajo Reservation of New Mexico and Arizona juts up into Utah's San Juan County in the southeast. Smaller reservations house the Southern Paiutes in southwestern Utah and the Gosiutes in west-central Utah.

Utah's small, permanent Spanish-speaking population numbers about 60,000. They identify themselves as Hispanic. In addition, thousands of migrant or seasonal Hispanic laborers are employed at agricultural jobs in the state each year. Utah's minorities include 9,225 blacks and about 5,000 Asians—Chinese and Japanese.

MORMONS AND GENTILES

Modern Utah is a cosmopolitan state, home to people of many faiths and cultural backgrounds. All non-Mormons, whatever their faith, were once known as Gentiles in Utah. As Utahans said, "Utah is the only place in the world where Jews are called Gentiles." Non-Mormons in Utah include about 60,000 Roman Catholics and 38,000 Protestants. Much smaller numbers attend Jewish synagogues, Greek Orthodox churches, and Buddhist temples. There is a Trappist monastery near Huntsville.

Many of Utah's Navajo people live in the spectacular Monument Valley area of the Navajo Reservation.

The state's past and present are closely tied to the Church of Jesus Christ of Latter-day Saints, commonly known as the Mormon church. Utah's population has been predominantly Mormon since 1847, when the first pioneers settled in Salt Lake City. In the towns and small cities, even on the streets of Salt Lake City, the people of Utah show a homogeneity (sameness) unique in the United States. The majority are of average height and have fair to medium-colored hair and skin. They reflect the heritage of the converts who came from the eastern and southern United States, Canada, and England, following their church to Utah.

Today, 70 percent of Utahans are Mormon. Although some Mormon dissenters have broken with the original church to form their own churches elsewhere, the Utah church is by far the largest. Headquartered in Salt Lake City, it claims a worldwide membership of about 7 million people, including nearly 1 million Utahans. Small numbers of Native Americans, blacks, and Japanese in Utah have been converted. The *Rama Mexicana* (Mexican Branch) was created in the 1920s to accommodate the growing number of Spanish-speaking Mormons.

THE MORMON FAITH

Mormons believe that revelations from God continue in the modern world. Thus, they believe, the Bible and the Mormon scriptures—*The Book of Mormon, Doctrine and Covenants,* and the *Pearl of Great Price*—all were divinely inspired. Together, the four books offer the foundation of the faith and creed of the church. In *Doctrine and Covenants,* Mormons find a practical, day-by-day guide to a healthy and righteous life within the church. One of its recommendations is that the faithful avoid tobacco, alcohol, coffee, and tea.

Baptism by immersion admits children eight years of age or older and adult converts into the church. In addition, living church members may be baptized as proxies, or stand-ins, for ancestors who died generations before the church was established. Because of this, genealogy (tracing one's relatives or "family tree") is very important to Mormons. Salt Lake City houses one of the world's best collections of genealogical records.

A bride and groom celebrate their union in the Mormon Temple, where they are sealed together for life and into the hereafter—as Mormons say, "for time and all eternity." Mormons believe in life after death, a final judgment, and the sacrament of the Lord's Supper.

Devout Mormons give a tithe (one-tenth of their income) to the church, and perform good works in the community. Worthy young men expect to devote twenty-four months of their lives to missionary work when they reach the age of nineteen. Young women may also be called to missionary work when they reach twenty-one years of age and are not married. Many of them travel to another country to preach, paying their own living expenses. Some retired couples are also called to do missionary work.

The Church of Jesus Christ of Latter-day Saints in Utah has no professional clergy. Instead, all worthy male members are ordained to the priesthood at age twelve. They progress through different offices and callings in the priesthood. Worthy male members nineteen years of age are ordained to the office of elder in the priesthood prior to receiving a mission call. There are other callings in the priesthood, such as bishop. Bishops preside over local congregations. Higher general authorities of the church direct church affairs throughout the world. Women do not enter the priesthood. The women of the church belong to the Relief Society, a compassionate service organization that is the largest women's organization in the world.

POLITICS

On the national level, Utah is politically conservative. Only seldom have Utah voters failed to support the Republican presidential ticket. Once was during the 1930s, when Democrat Franklin Delano Roosevelt's "New Deal" policies promised a way out of the Great Depression, which had affected Utah badly. Today, two of Utah's three representatives in the United States Congress, and both of its United States senators, are Republicans.

On the state level, Utahans are much less predictable. They often vote a split ticket, choosing some Republicans and some Democrats for office on the same ballot. In 1976, when Utah voters overwhelmingly supported Republican Gerald Ford as president, they also elected Scott Matheson, a Democrat, as their governor. Before the widespread use of automatic voting machines, election officials used to joke that it took longer to count those careful Utah choices than it took to count the ballots in any other state in the Union.

Chapter 4

THE BEGINNING

THE BEGINNING

*Once we lived in a land of plenty. But a great drought came
to dry up the streams. Plants withered and died, game birds
and animals fled. We prayed for help and the god Shinob
answered: "Have as much sense as the animals and birds. The
country is large and somewhere there is always food. If you
follow the animals and the birds they will lead you to it."*
—A Paiute legend

PREHISTORIC PEOPLES

The first peoples of Utah were Desert Culture hunters and
gatherers in the Great Basin. Danger Cave, near present-day
Wendover at the Utah-Nevada border, was occupied by Desert
Culture people beginning about twelve thousand years ago. They
lived in harmony with nature, moving with the seasons to collect
berries, grains, nuts, and medicinal plants.

Desert Culture peoples learned to find the best minerals with
which to make tools and weapons. They dried and ground seeds
and insects for food, made spears for hunting, and made baskets
for storage and carrying. Small family groups hunted rabbits,
rodents, and even insects. Sometimes several families joined
together to hunt larger animals such as antelope and sheep.

The Fremont Culture developed in Utah about A.D. 400.
Archaeologists believe that the Fremonts were Desert Culture
people who learned farming and building techniques from more-
advanced cultures in Mexico. Fremont sites are found throughout
Utah, north of the Colorado River, often in the top layer of an
older Desert Culture site.

An Anasazi cliff ruin along the Green River in Canyonlands National Park

Though Fremont people still depended heavily on food gathering, they learned to grow corn, squash, and beans to add to their diet. They built pit houses—shelters dug into the ground, lined with stone or plaster, and roofed over with tree limbs and brush. Caldwell Village in the Uinta Basin, with twenty pit houses, is one of the largest Fremont sites yet found.

South of the Colorado River, another food-growing culture flourished at the same time as the Fremont. They were the Anasazi, a Navajo word meaning the "Ancient Ones." The center of Anasazi culture was even farther south, in an area of present-day New Mexico and Arizona. The Anasazi depended more on farming to produce food, and grew their crops on irrigated fields. Anasazi pueblos, or villages, often housed several hundred people. The Anasazi built the first apartment houses, some of which were five stories high and were perched in cliff caves or on top of flat hills called mesas. Hovenweep, in southeastern Utah, is one of the largest and best-known Anasazi ruins in the state.

Newspaper Rock, near Monticello, displays ancient Indian symbols and figures called petroglyphs. The photograph on the left has been enhanced with color.

Both the Fremont and Anasazi cultures were known for their rock art. Everywhere they lived, they drew symbols and figures by painting or chipping pictures on canyon walls.

Mysteriously, both the Fremont peoples and the Anasazi had disappeared and faded into legend before Columbus reached North America. Their sites were abandoned in the late 1200s, perhaps because of a prolonged drought, or perhaps because aggressive newcomers entered the region. By the time the first major European expedition reached Utah in 1776, there were two established groups of Native Americans: Shoshonean-speakers and Navajos.

HISTORIC TRIBES

The Paiutes (or Pahutes), Gosiutes (or Goshutes), Utes, and Shoshones spoke dialects of the Shoshonean language. They entered the Utah region from southern California and northern Mexico at about the time the Fremont and Anasazi disappeared.

The Paiutes roamed southern Utah and parts of Arizona, Nevada, and California. They were hunters and gatherers who occasionally farmed small plots. They traveled in groups of just a few families, and recognized no strict tribal organization. Though horses became known through the Spanish conquerors of Mexico, the Paiutes were among the last to use horses except as the main course of an all-too-rare feast.

The Gosiutes lived in Utah's western deserts. Much like Desert Culture people long ago, they traveled in small family groups, cleverly foraging an inhospitable land for what food it offered. The Gosiutes were among the poorest of the Indians in the Southwest. Early explorers and settlers called them "Digger Indians" because of their basic diet of roots, seeds, and insects.

The Utes were the most numerous of Utah's historic Indian groups, and the first to make use of the Spaniards' horses. They became superb horsemen, and ranged over all of Utah in large bands hunting buffalo and other game. From the Spanish they also learned the value of slave trade. Soon they were raiding the weaker Paiutes and Gosiutes, carrying off women and children to sell as slaves in New Mexico.

Ute singers and storytellers created beautiful and inspiring tales of their gods, of the wonders of nature, and of the sometimes brave and sometimes foolish actions of human beings. Two famous Ute festivals—the spring Bear Dance and the summer Sun Dance—are still re-created every year.

Though the main area of Navajo culture was in Arizona and New Mexico, the fierce warriors took over the arid red-earth land of Utah's Four Corners region sometime during the early 1500s. The Navajos quickly learned the use of horses and sheep from the Spanish, and became a pastoral (herding) society. They wove beautiful woolen cloth and blankets and became masters at

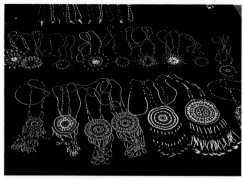

Navajos today are still a herding society and are still masters at jewelry making.

metalworking and jewelry making—crafts for which they are still famous today.

THE DOMÍNGUEZ-ESCALANTE EXPEDITION

Spaniards were the first Europeans in Utah. Francisco Atanasio Domínguez and Silvestre Vélez de Escalante were Franciscan friars (Catholic priests) who set out from Santa Fe, New Mexico, looking for an overland route to the Spanish missions in Monterey, California.

Their 2,000-mile (3,219-kilometer) journey began in July 1776, the same month and year as the signing of the Declaration of Independence. When they returned to Santa Fe 158 days later, General George Washington had just made his historic crossing of the Delaware River.

The Domínguez-Escalante party, on a 1776 expedition to the Spanish missions in California, kept a journal of their travels in Utah.

The two friars entered Utah near present-day Jensen, on the eastern border, and traveled west across the Wasatch Mountains. They reported that Utah Valley's size, good climate, and vegetation could support "as many Indian pueblos [as] New Mexico." Visiting a Ute encampment convinced them that the Indians were peaceful and ready for conversion to Christianity. Promising to return or to send other missionaries, they turned south. Foul weather, short supplies, and difficult terrain caused them to abandon the California quest and return to Santa Fe.

The Spanish never sent missionaries to the Indians as promised, and never sent settlers into Utah. But the *Domínguez-Escalante Journal* became the first written eyewitness report of Utah's peoples, its mountains and rivers, its plants and animal life. Bernardo Miera y Pacheco of the expedition drew up a map that would define the region for nearly a century. However, his map indicated a great river flowing from the Great Basin to the Pacific Ocean. Travelers trying to find that river in the desert paid for Miera's mistake with their lives.

Mountain men—brave and hardy fur traders such as the man shown at left in an Albert Bierstadt painting—hunted in Utah from the early 1800s until the 1840s. Etienne Provost (middle) and Jim Bridger (right) competed for Utah's prize pelts.

THE MOUNTAIN MEN

From the early 1800s until the 1840s, a few hundred brave and boisterous fur traders blazed their own trails through Utah, earning the name "Mountain Men." Beaver pelts were almost as good as gold—they sold for $10 in the St. Louis market. The pelts would be used to make beaver hats for fashionable men in European cities.

The following advertisement for William H. Ashley's American Fur Company appeared in an 1822 St. Louis newspaper: "To Enterprising Young Men: The subscriber wishes to engage one hundred young men to ascend the Missouri River to its source, there to be employed for one, two, or three years. . . ." Jim Bridger, Jedediah Strong Smith, and Jim Beckwourth started out with Ashley's company. The British Hudson's Bay Company, led by Peter Skene Ogden, competed for Utah furs. Kit Carson, Etienne Provost (or Provot), and Antoine Robidoux came up from Taos, New Mexico, on the same quest.

Alfred Jacob Miller's painting shows a spring *rendezvous*, at which fur traders, trappers, Indians, and company agents met to trade goods and to have some fun after a long, hard winter.

The men worked hard, alone or in small groups, trapping, skinning, and drying the pelts all fall and winter. In the spring, they met at a great *rendezvous*, a kind of annual trading fair. Trappers, Indians, and company agents bought, bartered, or exchanged pelts and supplies. Jim Beckwourth described the 1826 rendezvous at Ogden: "Mirth, songs, dancing, shouting, trading, running, jumping, singing, racing, target shooting, yarns, frolic, with all sorts of extravagances that white men or Indians could invent, were freely indulged in."

The mountain men moved on in the late 1840s, when the supply of game animals ran out and the value of a good pelt declined. They left behind a legacy of daring deeds and a growing knowledge of Utah's geography. Kit Carson became a famous guide in the region. Provost and Ogden gave their names to the cities of Provo and Ogden. Jim Bridger, credited as the first white man at the Great Salt Lake, is said to have tasted the water, spat it out, and announced that it must be the Pacific Ocean.

Jedediah Strong Smith was the first white man to cross Utah both from north to south and from west to east. In 1827, he crossed the desert and arrived at the Great Salt Lake with only a half-dead horse and a mule. "The balance of my horses I was compelled to eat as they gave out," he explained.

THE TRAIL BLAZERS

Crisscrossing the paths of the mountain men were government explorers and emigrants. Captain Benjamin Bonneville never entered Utah, despite the fact that prehistoric Lake Bonneville bears his name. In 1833, based on information provided by a small party of his men led by Joseph Walker, Bonneville prepared a map of the northern edge of the Great Basin.

The Bartleson-Bidwell party of 1841 was the first emigrant train to cross Utah. Bound for California via the famous Oregon Trail to the north, thirty-two men and one woman, Nancy Kelsey, decided to take a shortcut through Utah's Great Basin. If the route became too difficult, they planned to build boats and travel on that westward-flowing river shown on the Miera map. The realities of the desert forced them to abandon wagons, animals, and any possessions they could not carry. Ragged and weary, they straggled into California almost four months later.

John C. Frémont, one of the West's most famous government explorers, visited the Great Salt Lake Region in 1843-44, with Kit Carson as his guide. Frémont returned again in 1845. From his explorations, Frémont correctly identified the pattern of internal drainage, and was the first to use the name "Great Basin." He determined that Miera's map was wrong to show a great river connecting the basin and the ocean.

One of the great tragedies of westward travel was the ordeal of the 1846 Donner-Reed wagon train. Without benefit of Frémont's records, those emigrants chose Utah as a shortcut to the golden land of California. They spent three weeks hacking out a wagon road through the Wasatch Mountains and down into the basin, and more weeks inching across the desert.

The Utah passage cost so much in time, energy, and equipment that the Donner-Reed party became snowbound in the Sierra Nevada Mountains. Many died of hunger and exposure. Some turned to cannibalism, eating the flesh of their dead companions. Only forty-four of the eighty-seven emigrants who started out lived through that terrible winter to reach California.

Less than one year later, the first of the Mormon wagon trains traveled through the Wasatch in the tracks of the Donner-Reed wagons. The history of Utah was about to change forever.

THE SEARCH FOR ZION

In Utah, the 1820s was the heyday of the mountain men, a time of excitement and daring. In New York, it was a time of great religious upheaval. Fiery preachers denounced established churches. New sects sprang up like sown wheat. Fourteen-year-old Joseph Smith was inspired by visions promising that he alone could restore the true church of Christ. He told his family and friends that an angel of the Lord had guided him to a set of golden plates buried in the Hill Cumorah, near Palmyra, New York. With the aid of further visions, Smith translated the plates and published *The Book of Mormon* in 1830. That same year, the Church of Jesus Christ of Latter-day Saints was born. Its members became known as Latter-day Saints, Saints, or Mormons.

Impassioned Mormon preachers spread the word throughout the United States, Canada, and Europe. The church grew rapidly and Mormons developed into a closely knit group that excluded outsiders. Their attitude and their success aroused resentment. Church leaders were attacked and church property was destroyed. Mormons fled from New York to Ohio to Missouri. Hounded out of Missouri, they founded Nauvoo, on the banks of the Mississippi River in Illinois.

Soon Nauvoo was growing at a faster pace than even Chicago. Joseph Smith declared his intention to seek the United States presidency. Smith's ambition, combined with Mormon prosperity in Illinois, provoked still more violent attacks. An angry mob murdered Joseph Smith in 1844. Frightened and embittered, the Mormons resolved to move out of the United States, beyond the western frontier. They chose Brigham Young as their leader. And he chose far-off Salt Lake Valley, uncharted and unwanted by other Americans—except the thousands of Native Americans who called Utah home. It would be a Mormon Zion, a gathering place for the Saints.

More than ten thousand Saints marched west from Nauvoo early in 1846. Brigham Young organized them into small companies. Advance parties built temporary shelters and sowed crops for those who would follow. A chain of Mormon camps stretched across the plains, pointing like an arrow toward Utah.

On July 22, 1847, a Mormon advance party of about 170 people entered Salt Lake Valley. Two days later, Young joined the advance group and finalized the decision to settle there. The Mormon pioneers had traveled 111 weary days to reach Salt Lake Valley from their winter camp at Council Bluffs, Iowa.

Chapter 5
THE MORMON ERA

THE MORMON ERA

A sterile desert, bleak and bare,
Was Utah when our fathers came,
The Redman's shout, the howl of beasts,
The only sound on hill and plain.
And yet when gazing from the height,
The leader of that sturdy band,
Stirred every heart to songs of joy,
As viewing he exclaimed:
This is the place, This is the place...
—"Ode to Utah," by A.M. Durnham

THE BUILDING OF ZION

Brigham Young, weakened from fever and the long journey, had to be helped out of the wagon for his first sight of Salt Lake Valley. It was July 24, 1847. Eagerly, the rest of the Mormon pioneers awaited his reaction. "This is the place," he is said to have proclaimed, "this is the right place." The weary travelers sighed. The difficult trip was over. But could this dry and isolated land be the Saints' Kingdom of God on Earth, their Zion?

Mormon Zion was to be a self-sufficient agricultural community, made green and rich by irrigation. The very day they arrived, the Mormons began irrigating and plowing. Everyone worked in the fields, including the children, the three women, and the three black slaves among the pioneers. One month later, they could report: "[We] broke, watered, planted, and sowed upwards of 100 acres with various kinds of seeds."

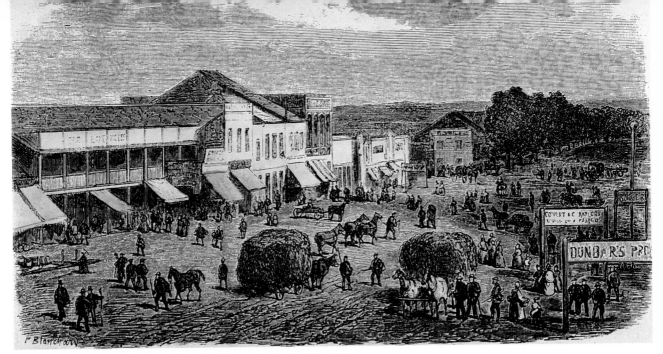

A street in Salt Lake City as it looked in 1871

Other Mormon caravans followed them into the valley. In the first year, they laid out Salt Lake City in 135 ten-acre (4-hectare) blocks, reserving a site at the north end for the temple. Explorations of nearby valleys began.

According to Mormon legend, disaster threatened in 1848 when a horde of crickets blackened the sky and attacked the crop. As despairing pioneers watched and prayed, swarms of gulls soared up from the Great Salt Lake. Darting through the air, they gobbled up the crickets "by the thousands of tons," according to one report. With enough of the crop saved to get them through the winter, the Mormons gave thanks for the miracle of the gulls.

In a few short years, Salt Lake Valley farms were thriving. Mormon settlements expanded into neighboring valleys. The remarkable achievements of the pioneers resulted from their exceptional spirit of cooperation. Directed by church leaders, they gave their energies first to such public works as irrigation projects and community building, and only then to their personal needs.

These newly converted Mormons were among the nearly four thousand "handcart company" pioneers who walked east on the Mormon Trail between 1856 and 1860.

Even as they were building homes and planting crops, Mormon men were often sent on proselytizing missions by their church leaders. Their pioneer wives stayed behind. It was their mission to care for the young children and the aging parents and to grow or forage food for the family. Others might be "called" as families to establish new settlements.

THE HANDCART COMPANIES

Building a Mormon stronghold in Utah required dedication and the labor of thousands of the faithful. A Perpetual Emigrating Fund Company was established in 1849 to provide loans to those too poor to pay their own way to Utah. As each immigrant repaid the loan, funds were available for others. Thousands of converts from the United States and the British Isles were eager to "come to the place of gathering, as doves flock to their windows before a storm." By 1854, nearly twenty-two thousand Mormons had come to America from Europe.

And with the faithful make a start,
To cross the plains with your handcart.
For some must push and some must pull,
As we go marching up the hill.
So merrily on the way we go,
Until we reach the Valley.

"The Handcart Song" refers to the nearly four thousand people who walked the Mormon Trail with handcarts between 1856 and 1860. Personal possessions were limited to just over fifteen pounds (seven kilograms) for each traveler and piled onto handcarts to be pushed and tugged along the road. Five companies crossed in the first year, but the last two started out late and were trapped short of their goal by early snows. Some two hundred people died from freezing and starvation before a relief column from the valley could ride to their aid.

Mary Ann Hafen was a child in 1860 when she went to Utah with the last of the handcart companies. Her family left England in May, reached the Mormon Trail in July, and caught their first glimpse of Salt Lake Valley that September. She remembered: "There were six to our cart. Father and Mother pulled it; Rosie (two years old) rode; John (nine) and I (six) walked. Sometimes, when it was downhill, they let me ride, too. . . . Mother's feet [grew] so swollen that she could not wear shoes, but had to wrap her feet with cloth."

CHALLENGES IN ZION

Brigham Young argued that it was "cheaper to feed and clothe [the Indians] than to fight them." Against the precedent being set everywhere else in the West, Mormons were urged to give food and other supplies to the Indians and to treat them fairly. Jacob Hamblin, a dedicated and effective Mormon missionary to the

Indians, made up a set of rules to guide him. Rule number one was: "I never talk anything but the truth to them." But the truth was that Mormons spread beyond Salt Lake Valley, plowing up the wild plant foods and occupying the sites with the best access to water.

Ute Chief Walkara (known as Walker) befriended the Mormons at first. Soon he came to resent their expanding settlements and their efforts to stop the Utes' profitable slave trade with New Mexico. The Walker War, one of Utah's few Indian wars, began as a series of skirmishes in 1853 and ended in 1854. During the unrest, Captain John W. Gunnison and seven of his men, all conducting a survey of possible railroad routes in Utah, were killed by Indians.

Meanwhile, two events that occurred outside Utah brought "Gentiles" (non-Mormons) into the area and reawakened anti-Mormon hostility. These were the California Gold Rush and the Mexican War. More than fifteen thousand gold hunters arrived in Salt Lake City each year from 1849 to 1851. Traveling through Utah, they traded surplus household goods, clothes, even machinery and tools for food and fresh animals needed to complete the journey. Gentiles made the deals, but complained bitterly at Mormon prices.

Although Salt Lake Valley was a Mexican possession when the Saints arrived, one year later the Saints were back in the United States. War between Mexico and the United States (1846-48) cost Mexico most of its territories north of the Rio Grande, including the new Mormon settlements.

The Mormons asked Congress to approve a new state composed of present-day Utah and Nevada as well as parts of Arizona, Idaho, Wyoming, Colorado, Oregon, New Mexico, and California. They planned to name it Deseret, from the word for "honeybee"

A Mormon family, 1884

in *The Book of Mormon*, and they wanted Brigham Young as governor. Congress rejected both the name and the boundaries of Deseret.

Instead, Congress created Utah Territory, named for the Utes, in 1850. It appointed Brigham Young as governor, and named both Mormon and non-Mormon territorial officials. Many of the new officials distrusted the Mormons, who looked to Brigham Young and other church figures for leadership instead of depending on federal officeholders in the territory. They accused the Mormons of treason against the United States and hinted that the church directed or accepted the murder of its enemies. Most of all, they accused the Mormon men of enslaving Mormon women.

POLYGAMY

Polygamy, or plural marriage (one man taking more than one wife), was publicly announced as church practice in Utah in 1852, though Mormons had practiced it for about ten years before that.

Estimates about the number of Mormon men who took more than one wife vary from 2 to 10 percent. Most of Mormon society defended the idea. The rest of the country was shocked, angered, or saddened.

The first wife did not have to agree to a second marriage, though she was often asked anyway, and the church had to approve. Plural marriages, like all Mormon marriages, were "sealed for eternity."

Mary Ann Hafen, who walked to Utah with a handcart in 1860, grew up to be a plural wife, one of four. Her husband was eighty-nine years old in 1927 when he numbered his descendants at 211, including 27 children, 131 grandchildren, and 53 great-grandchildren.

THE UTAH WAR

By the time the Mormons had been in the valley ten years, they had founded Salt Lake City, Ogden, Provo, and some one hundred other towns. Utah Territory now contained nearly forty thousand people. On July 24, 1857, just as the Mormons were celebrating their tenth anniversary in Utah, word came that federal troops were marching against them.

The national press had delighted in reporting the scandalous Mormon practice of polygamy. Porter Rockwell, bodyguard first of Joseph Smith and then of Brigham Young, was depicted as a near legendary "avenging angel" who murdered at will Gentiles and dissenting Mormons targeted by the church. There were rumors that Mormons had caused the deaths of Captain Gunnison and his men. Federal officials returning from Utah Territory claimed that the Mormons were rebelling against the United States by interfering with Utah territorial government.

Such strong and widespread resentment against the Mormons persuaded newly elected President James Buchanan to act. He sent an army of twenty-five hundred men and a new federal governor to Utah. Brigham Young responded by calling up the Utah militia to defend Mormon lives and Mormon beliefs.

The Mormons waged a guerrilla war against the advancing army. They torched likely campsites, forcing the United States soldiers, weary from a day's march, to put out fires each night before they could rest. Without a single killing, the army was forced to halt in Wyoming, where it made a winter camp and awaited the arrival of Colonel Albert Sidney Johnston.

Meanwhile, in Salt Lake Valley, settlers were directed to abandon their homes and farms and prepare to evacuate the northern half of the state, and perhaps all of Utah. Salt Lake City was boarded up. Many homes were stuffed with well-dried hay, and a few men were designated to stay behind to burn the houses and fields if the army arrived. Mormons were called in from far-flung settlements that would be difficult to defend. Together with the Salt Lake Valley settlers, all moved south. In all, forty thousand Mormons left their homes.

National sentiment temporarily swung in favor of the resolute Mormons. A June 1858 editorial in the *New York Times* described the Utah War as a "singular mixture of farce and tragedy," adding: "Whatever our opinions may be of Mormon morals or Mormon manners, there can be no question that this voluntary abandonment by forty thousand people of homes created by a wonderful industry in the midst of trackless wastes . . . is something from which [no one] . . . can withhold his admiration."

President Buchanan began to regret his hasty action. Thomas Kane, an influential Philadelphian and a friend of the Mormons since Nauvoo times, arranged a meeting between Alfred

The major disaster of the Utah War was the Mountain Meadows Massacre, in which Indians and Mormons killed more than one hundred non-Mormon emigrants whose wagon train was traveling across southern Utah.

Cumming, the new federal governor, and Brigham Young. President Buchanan offered the Mormons amnesty if they accepted Governor Cumming and allowed Johnston's troops to be stationed in Utah. The Mormons agreed, and returned to their homes in the summer of 1858.

The Utah War resulted in one major disaster, the Mountain Meadows Massacre. Although the full story of the events leading up to it are clouded, the passions aroused by the invading army led to the massacre of some 120 Gentiles. They were killed in September 1857 as their wagon train traveled through southern Utah. Though the initial attack was made by Indians, Mormons became involved in the final slaughter. Indian missionary Jacob Hamblin participated in the killing. So did church leader John D. Lee, the only man later convicted of the crime.

THE END OF ISOLATION

The years following the Utah War saw increased attention to travel and communication. The Pony Express sent daring riders and swift horses to deliver the mail across the West. A letter from Washington, D.C., reached Salt Lake City in seven days by Pony

Express. A letter sent from Salt Lake City to California arrived in four days. The Overland Telegraph, the world's first transcontinental telegraph line, was completed in 1861. Now that every city and town linked by telegraph could be in instant communication, the Pony Express came to a sudden end, a year and a half after it began.

Johnston's army left Utah after three years, called away to service in the Civil War. But telegraph and mail routes needed protection. California volunteers, under the command of Colonel Patrick Connor, arrived in Utah. Connor's job was to keep an eye on the Mormons, whom the federal government did not trust, and to protect the territory and control the Indians. Instead, Connor attacked the Indians at any provocation, from minor skirmishes with roving bands to the 1863 Battle of Bear River, where he massacred between two hundred and four hundred Shoshones.

Congress created the Uintah Reservation for Utes in 1864, and demanded that the Indians give up all other lands and move immediately. Dissatisfaction with the reservation treaties was a major cause of Utah's last big Indian war, the Ute-Black Hawk War, which broke out in central Utah in 1865. Raiding and hostilities had diminished by 1868, and the Utes gradually moved onto the reservation. Navajo resistance to white settlers in southeastern Utah was resolved in 1884 by the creation of another reservation. No longer would Indians roam freely in Utah.

Headstrong and hot tempered, Connor was also fiercely anti-Mormon. He ordered his men to prospect Utah's mountains for mineral wealth. A mining boom, he reasoned, would bring in large numbers of Gentiles and break Mormon economic control in Utah. Although Connor's men made several strikes in Bingham Canyon, Utah's mining boom awaited the development of railroads to transport the heavy ore.

In May 1869, the tracks of the Union Pacific and Central Pacific railroads met at Promontory Summit, Utah. A golden spike was driven to complete the transcontinental railroad that linked the two coasts of the United States.

Two competing railroads were already racing to fulfill a national dream—a transcontinental railroad linking the two coasts of the United States. Union Pacific's Irish work gangs laid track from the east across the plains, fighting Indians and the weather. Central Pacific's Chinese workers started from the west, conquering mountain barriers and desert. They met at Promontory Summit, Utah. On a cold and icy May day in 1869, telegraph lines around the world hummed with the message: "The last rail is laid. The last spike is driven. The Pacific railroad is finished." A golden spike completed the final link.

Mormon leaders were heavily involved in extending railroad and telegraph lines everywhere in Utah. Gentiles, too, rushed in for railroad jobs. Corinne, the first non-Mormon Utah town, was founded on the Bear River in 1868. Called the "Burg on the Bear," it attracted hardworking and hard-living railroaders, freighters, and miners. Corinne was the base for the anti-Mormon political party, the Liberals. The Mormons had their own People's party.

The town petitioned Congress, unsuccessfully, to make Corinne the Utah capital instead of Salt Lake City.

With the arrival of railroads, mining became vastly more important and profitable. For a decade, gold and silver strikes created boomtowns one day, and ghost towns the next, when the ore petered out.

Utah's silver and gold rush did not last long, but it led the way to what would become basic and prosperous industries: lead, coal, and copper mining. Asians, Welsh, and Scandinavians worked the mines in the 1870s. Italians, Greeks, and other "new immigrants" from eastern and southern Europe joined them in the 1880s and 1890s. By the 1880s, the Gentiles had established their own churches and private schools in Utah and were demanding free public schools to replace Mormon-dominated schools.

TOWARD STATEHOOD

Utah continued to grow. Between 1860 and 1870, the population increased by more than 115 percent. By 1880, nearly 150,000 people lived in Utah Territory. St. George and other towns were settled in the southwest.

Noted explorer Major John Wesley Powell was a key figure in opening up the Colorado Plateau in the southeast. There, in the 1870s, settlers began taking up lands promised to the Ute Reservation Indians, but the population remained sparse.

Brigham Young died in 1877. His strength and vision had brought 100,000 Mormons to Utah. He had directed the settlement of more than four hundred communities and had seen them linked together with a network of railroad and telegraph lines.

Utah was ready for statehood. Its population, mineral wealth, and strategic location on the major transportation networks of the nation all justified statehood. But Congress was reluctant. Utah would be a problem until Mormon dominance and Mormon polygamy ceased. The tension continued.

Though Congress had passed an antibigamy law in 1862, it did little to end the practice of polygamy. Twenty years later, the Edmunds Act imposed heavy fines on polygamists and took away their rights — and the rights of people who merely believed in polygamy — to vote and hold office. Caught and brought before a court, polygamists were convicted, fined, and jailed. More than twelve thousand were disenfranchised; thirteen hundred were jailed. Church leaders with more than one wife went into hiding and advised their membership to do the same.

The final blow to polygamy came with the Edmunds-Tucker Act of 1887, which stripped the church of its property. The nearly bankrupt church finally gave in. Wilford Woodruff, church president, issued a manifesto in 1890: "... I now publicly declare that my advice to the Latter-day Saints is to refrain from contracting any marriage forbidden by the law of the land." Quietly, the church gave in on other sources of conflict. It dissolved its People's party and encouraged Mormons to join national political parties. It ceased to oppose free public schools. It gave up its efforts to establish a self-sufficient communitarian economy and became more and more capitalistic. In general, it sought to join the mainstream of American life.

Utah had petitioned the United States Congress six times for statehood and six times had been denied. Finally, on January 4, 1896, it was admitted to the Union as the forty-fifth state. Its constitution prohibited polygamy ever after, although existing polygamous marriages were not dissolved, and it gave women the right to vote. With Mormon leader Heber M. Wells as its first governor, Utah looked forward to a new era and a new century.

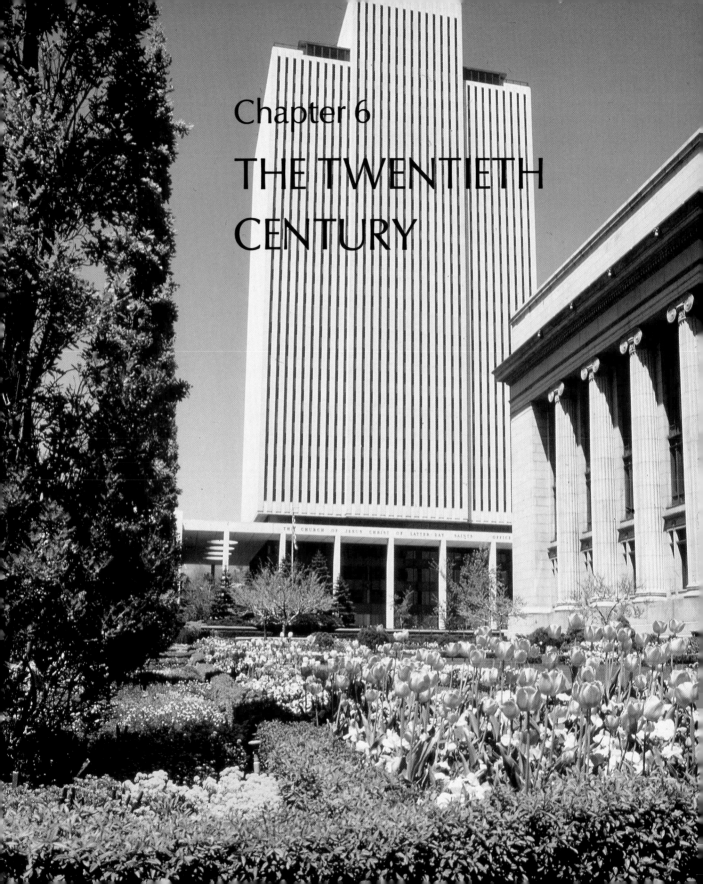

Chapter 6
THE TWENTIETH
CENTURY

THE TWENTIETH CENTURY

*I don't think the words exist to convey what it's like
to see the earth from space. . . . The sheer beauty of the
earth and the excitement of being in a position to see it
made this the greatest experience in my life.*

—Jake Garn, a Mormon representing Utah, on becoming
the first United States senator ever to go on a
spaceflight mission while still in office, 1985

UTAH ENTERS MAINSTREAM AMERICA

Crowds jammed the intersection of Main and South Temple
streets in Salt Lake City to watch the unveiling of the Brigham
Young Monument. It was July 24, 1897, fifty years after the
Mormons entered Salt Lake Valley and eighteen months after
Utah became a state. An era had ended.

The rest of the nation still viewed Utah with suspicion. Hints of
scandal and the old Utah War charges of treason and polygamy
were being kept alive. Congress refused to seat Brigham H.
Roberts, a polygamist, elected to the United States House of
Representatives in 1898, and Reed L. Smoot, elected to the United
States Senate in 1903. Roberts bowed out, but Smoot fought for
years during much-publicized hearings. He won, and went on to
serve Utah in the Senate for almost thirty years.

Mormon women ran for political office in Utah during the
earliest years of statehood. Martha Hughes Cannon defeated her

This cabin belonged to George Parker, more commonly known as Butch Cassidy, a notorious Utah bank robber, highwayman, and cattle and horse thief.

own husband to become the first female state senator in the nation, in 1896. A doctor and a plural wife, her comment about polygamy delighted the national press: "If her husband has four wives, [the plural wife] has three weeks of freedom every single month." Mary W. Howard, one of the first female mayors in the nation, and her all-female town council in Kanab were not so widely quoted when they debated local taxes and bridge building.

Utah was determined to become an all-American state. It elected Thomas Kearns to the United States Senate in 1901. Publisher of the *Salt Lake Tribune* and an outspoken critic of Mormons, Kearns had become a millionaire when he made a rich silver strike in Park City. Utah broke new ground politically by electing Simon Bamberger governor in 1917. He was the state's first Democratic, first non-Mormon, and first Jewish governor.

Because the railroads provided access to distant markets, cattle and sheep ranching prospered in the canyons of southern and southeastern Utah. Hundreds of western stories depicted the adventures of Utah's cowboys, Indians, and bandits. Butch Cassidy, a Utahan born of Mormon parents, operated with his "Robber's Roost" gang from a hiding place in the San Rafael Swell

The early Mormon settlers used irrigation to establish thriving farms throughout the bare, dry Salt Lake Valley. By 1900, thousands of acres of grain and sugar beets were being grown with dry-farming methods.

area between present-day Green River and Hanksville. Cassidy became a legendary Robin Hood figure, noted for daring deeds and a reluctance to kill his victims.

Agriculture changed. In the 1880s, David Broadhead of Nephi had been charged with perjury for claiming in court that wheat could be raised without irrigation. He went home and nailed up a sign: Perjury Farm. Twenty years later, thousands of acres of grain and sugar beets were being grown in Utah with dry-farming methods. Processed beet sugar became Utah's major manufactured product, second only to metals.

In 1913, Strawberry Reservoir, the state's largest water-diversion project, was completed. It brought water from the Colorado Basin to the Great Basin, adding greatly to the farm acreage that could be irrigated.

TROUBLED TIMES

Oh, mothers and wives of the miners,
Who perished so suddenly there,
Did you give them a loving embrace that morn?
Did you bid them "Goodbye" with a prayer?

This folk song was written in the wake of the nation's most devastating mining disaster. At 10:25 on the morning of May 1, 1900, at the Pleasant Valley Coal Company's Scofield mine, there was a low thud and a sudden trembling of the ground. Experienced miners at the site could tell there had been an underground explosion. More than three hundred men and boys were working in the mine at the time. The explosion claimed the lives of two hundred workers and would-be rescuers, more than any other mining disaster up to that time, and spurred the growth of the labor movement in Utah.

Silver, lead, and coal mines employed thousands of workers, most of whom were new immigrants. Old-time Utahans began to associate union activists and labor unrest with "foreigners." Italian and Yugoslav coal miners went on strike in Carbon County's coalfields in 1903. The strike was put down by the National Guard and the workers were replaced by Greek laborers. In 1912, nearly five thousand Greek, Italian, Cornish, and Japanese miners walked off their jobs at the "world's biggest hole in the ground," the huge copper mine at Bingham Canyon. Mine owner Daniel Jackling, backed by the National Guard, imported thousands of strikebreakers from Mexico and elsewhere.

The execution of Joe Hill in 1915 was Utah's most notorious labor incident. Hill was a Swedish immigrant and a member of the radical labor union, the Industrial Workers of the World (IWW, or "Wobblies"). Accused of murdering a Salt Lake City

Strikes plagued Utah's mining companies during the early 1900s. In 1912, nearly five thousand workers walked off their jobs at the "world's biggest hole in the ground," the huge copper mine at Bingham Canyon.

grocer and his son, Hill was put on trial. He did not defend himself, even though the evidence was circumstantial. Spellbound workers and social activists around the world followed the trial. When he was found guilty and executed by a firing squad, they declared that Joe Hill was a martyr of labor and that Utah was a corrupt and biased state. As a last slap at the state, ashes from Joe Hill's cremated body were scattered in every state in the Union except Utah. Hill's exit line, just before he was executed, was classic: "Don't waste time mourning. Organize!"

World War I created a heavy demand for Utah's mining and agricultural products. Prosperity made it possible for workers to win such concessions as a workmen's compensation law and the right to organize. World War I also put an end to any lingering doubts about Utah's patriotism. Many of the state's young people enlisted in the service. Others stayed home to provide the metals and produce needed by the United States and the Allies.

FROM DOLLAR TO DOLE

The end of World War I brought a reduced market for Utah products, and freight costs skyrocketed. It was a disaster for the

Strikers failed to gain new safety regulations even after the
1924 Castle Gate coal-mine explosion cost 127 lives. Boys as
young as this nine-year-old Finnish child died in the disaster.

state. By the early 1920s, most of Utah's mines were closed and the
state had one of the highest unemployment rates in the nation.

When Utah workers joined the nationwide coal-miners' strike
in 1922, the National Guard arrived once again. The strike failed
in Utah. Workers could not even get new safety regulations when
an explosion cost 127 lives at the Castle Gate coal mine in 1924.

Prejudice, along with unemployment and hard times, fueled
hostility. The Ku Klux Klan terrorized minority groups
throughout the nation during the 1920s. In Utah, the Klan rode at
night in mining and railroading towns. In Salt Lake City, blacks
and immigrants, whose skin color, customs, or language set them
apart, woke up at night to white-sheeted Klansmen with burning
crosses. Young Greek children went to bed with amulets (magic
charms) around their necks to protect them from both evil spells
and the Klan.

Utah's 1920s depression slid all too quickly into the nationwide
Great Depression of the 1930s. A third of the state's banks failed
after the 1929 stock-market crash. Mining and refining companies
went out of business. Farms ended up on the auction block.

During the Great Depression of the 1930s, these Salt Lake City teachers made sure that their students had at least one good meal a day, even when they had to purchase food with money from their own pockets.

Utah was one of the hardest-hit states in the nation. One Utahan in every three was unemployed by 1933. One in every three needed welfare—jobs, food, clothing, and cash. Thousands of Utahans migrated to other states between 1920 and 1940. Minority workers suffered greatly. Their jobs had been concentrated in mining and agriculture. Almost half a million Hispanic workers returned to Mexico from Utah in the 1930s.

The depression inspired the formation of the Mormon church's Welfare Plan, which was helpful in Utah. President Franklin Delano Roosevelt's New Deal program brought jobs and relief to the entire nation. Utahans went to work on public projects at federal government expense. They built roads and bridges. They built three hundred public buildings. They worked on water- and soil-reclamation projects. The New Deal programs—and the onset of World War II—put Utah on the road to recovery.

THE WORLD WAR II BOOM

When the world went to war again, Utah was a choice site for United States defense and military installations. It has an inland

More than eight thousand Japanese Americans from the West Coast were relocated to the Topaz camp in Millard County, where they lived from 1942 to 1945.

location, excellent transportation and communication facilities, mineral wealth, and open spaces. During World War II, ten military and defense installations opened up nearly fifty thousand jobs in the state. Another fifty thousand Utahans found work in construction and services related to the war effort.

Major arsenals at Ogden, Clearfield, and Tooele prepared and distributed the supplies of war. Isolated Dugway Proving Ground tested chemical and flamethrowing weapons. Kearns and Hill air bases were built. Wendover Army Air Base arose in the Great Salt Lake Desert. The Enola Gay crew, who dropped the first atomic bomb on Hiroshima, Japan, were trained in Wendover.

The Japanese attack on Pearl Harbor on December 7, 1941, provoked national rage at all people of Japanese ancestry. Executive Order 9066 passed in 1942. It forced Japanese Americans to evacuate California and the Pacific Coast and live in ''relocation'' camps for the rest of the war. One such camp, Topaz, was located in arid land in Millard County, Utah. Its low, tar-paper-covered barracks, surrounded by barbed wire, were home to more than eight thousand Japanese Americans between 1942 and 1945. With dry wit, the evacuees called it ''Topaz, the Jewel of the Desert.''

By the 1960s, seven of every ten Utahans lived in Salt Lake City (above), Ogden, Provo, or other urban areas where industries and military bases were located.

A TIME OF CHANGE

After World War II, Utah would never be the same. Its population jumped 25 percent between 1940 and 1950 and nearly 30 percent between 1950 and 1960. Agriculture and mining, the big employers of the first half of the century, occupied only a small part of the labor force. Utah had become industrialized. The federal government had become a major employer. By the 1960s, seven of every ten Utahans lived in Ogden, Salt Lake City, Provo, or other urban areas where most of the state's industries and military bases were located.

Utah returned to Republican, conservative politics. Governor J. Bracken Lee, one of Utah's most colorful figures during the postwar years, was an outspoken conservative. He welcomed federal spending and vigorously rejected federal regulation. In the midst of a global "cold war," he often claimed to be more worried about the government in Washington, D.C., than the one in

During the tourism boom that began in the 1960s, ski resorts such as this one near Alta opened in the Wasatch Range.

Moscow. He cut budgets and taxes in the state, waged war with the Internal Revenue Service, and banned the celebration of United Nations Day in Utah. His popularity dimmed in the late 1950s, but by the 1960s he was back on the political scene as a three-term mayor of Salt Lake City. At the same time, Ezra Taft Benson, secretary of agriculture under President Dwight D. Eisenhower and a leading figure in the Mormon church, publicly championed ultraconservative political causes.

PROGRESS VS. THE ENVIRONMENT

A tourism boom in the 1960s created jobs in hotels, restaurants, and other service industries. Ski resorts opened in the Wasatch Range, offering recreation opportunities to Utah's city dwellers as well as to out-of-state vacationers. Thousands of other visitors were attracted by Utah's vast expanses of national forestland and its spectacular national parks and monuments.

Utahans learned that industrialization and progress can be very costly. Air pollution is a statewide problem. With so many industries and so many workers commuting in automobiles up and down the Wasatch Front urban area, residents began to experience raw throats and red, watery eyes every time temperature changes led to an air inversion. A statewide effort to halt pollution, beginning in 1969, has had some success. However, even in the late 1980s, estimates suggest that pollution has cut visibility by 30 to 40 percent even in such remote areas as Bryce Canyon National Park.

Utah will have to decide how to balance jobs and progress with environmental concerns. A plan to build a nuclear-waste dump near Moab and Canyonlands National Park aroused strong feelings in 1987. Environmentalist Del Smith argued that "tourism is Utah's second-largest industry . . . unlike feast-or-famine, boom-or-bust mineral development, a tourist industry is reliable." Utah Congressman James V. Hansen favored the dump site: "Sure, there would be some buildings and a chain-link fence, but you can't eliminate the growth of the West to placate a few tourists."

CHALLENGES AND PROMISES

Minorities make up only a small portion of Utah's population. As late as the 1950s, prominent black entertainers such as Harry Belafonte, Nat "King" Cole, and Marian Anderson appeared before white audiences but were denied rooms in white hotels. Conditions improved after the Civil Rights Movement of the 1960s. In 1978, the Church of Jesus Christ of Latter-day Saints began accepting black men to the priesthood.

Scandal rocked Utah's majority Mormon population in the late

1980s. Investigation into the 1985 pipe-bombing deaths of two people in Salt Lake City involved Mark Hoffman, a member of the Mormon church. Hoffman, convicted of the killings, had been trying to extort money for brilliantly forged documents that cast doubt on church founder Joseph Smith and the origins of *The Book of Mormon.*

When Addam Swapp and his family of fourteen stood off the police in a two-week siege at Marion in 1988, headlines around the nation once again screamed "Polygamy!" Swapp was convicted of bombing a local Mormon church in a fantastic scheme to revenge the 1979 killing of another polygamist. One officer was killed. Swapp was seriously wounded, but he was brought to trial amid publicity that embarrassed the whole state.

Happier headlines announced gains in medical research. In 1982, at Salt Lake City's University of Utah medical center, Barney Clark became the first person in the world to receive an artificial heart implant. Six years later, federal officials approved human testing for the Jarvik 100, successor to the original Jarvik 7 heart implanted in Clark. University of Utah scientists have used the Mormon church's extensive genealogical resources to trace and study generations of medical history within single families. In 1988, they identified the chemical code responsible for a form of inherited colon cancer.

New and diverse industries in computer services and alternative energy systems offer promise for the future. Utah takes pride in its past, in the contributions of its Native Americans, in its minority groups, and in its Mormon majority. Committed to education, increasingly responsive to environmental concerns, eager to provide better jobs, better homes, and the best possible standard of living for its people, Utah looks forward to the twenty-first century with hope and confidence.

Chapter 7

GOVERNMENT AND THE ECONOMY

GOVERNMENT AND THE ECONOMY

GOVERNMENT

Utah's state constitution was ratified in November 1895, just two months before President Grover Cleveland proclaimed Utah the forty-fifth state. Utah was the second state (following Wyoming) to give women the right to vote. An amendment to the constitution in 1900 gave the people of Utah the right to legislate directly through the process of initiative and referendum.

The government of Utah, like that of the United States, is divided into three main branches. The legislative branch is responsible for making the laws; the executive branch carries out the laws; and the judicial branch interprets the laws and tries cases.

The executive department is headed by the governor, who is elected to a four-year term. The governor has the power to appoint many important state officials, to approve or veto (reject) proposed laws, and, in times of emergency, to call out the state militia. Other important officers in the executive department are the lieutenant governor, the attorney general, the state auditor, and the state treasurer, all of whom are elected by the people to serve four-year terms. If the governorship becomes vacant, the lieutenant governor serves as governor. Since Utah does not have a secretary of state, most of the duties of that office are performed by the lieutenant governor.

The Utah legislature consists of a twenty-nine-member senate and a seventy-five-member house of representatives. State senators serve four-year terms and state representatives serve two-year terms. The legislature decides which proposals, or bills, will become law, but before a bill becomes law it must be signed by the governor. If the governor refuses to sign a bill, and two-thirds of the members of the legislature vote to override the veto, the bill becomes a law even without the governor's signature.

The legislature, working with the governor, decides how the state will spend its money. Grants from the federal government and a sales tax on purchased goods are Utah's largest sources of revenue. An income tax on the earnings of workers is also an important source of state funds.

Utah's judicial branch consists of a supreme court, district courts, circuit courts, and justices of the peace. There is also a statewide system of juvenile courts. The supreme court has five members who serve staggered ten-year terms. Every two years, a new justice joins the court, and the justice with only two years left to serve becomes the chief justice. Members are appointed by the governor, but they must be approved by the voters in the following general election. The supreme court can declare state laws unconstitutional, and it hears appeals from the lower courts.

EDUCATION

Utah's earliest schools were run by the Mormon church. The constitution of 1895 called for free public schools. Today, approximately 40 percent of the state budget is spent on educating the more than 230,000 elementary students and 140,000 secondary students who attend Utah's public schools. Utah is among the national leaders in the percentage of school-age children attending

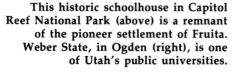
This historic schoolhouse in Capitol
Reef National Park (above) is a remnant
of the pioneer settlement of Fruita.
Weber State, in Ogden (right), is one
of Utah's public universities.

school, the percentage of students graduating from high school,
and the percentage of students who go on to college.

The University of Deseret, founded in 1850, changed its name to
the University of Utah in 1892. Today, more than 24,000 students
are enrolled at its sprawling campus in Salt Lake City. They study
everything from archaeology to zoology. It was at the University
of Utah that much of the early work in the development of the
artificial heart was conducted. The University's Howard Hughes
Medical Institute became a national leader in cancer research in
the late 1980s.

Utah's other public-supported universities include Utah State
University in Logan, Weber State in Ogden, and Southern Utah
State College in Cedar City. Two-year state colleges, scattered
around the state, include Dixie College in St. George, the College
of Eastern Utah in Price, and Snow College in Ephraim. Salt Lake
City and Orem have two-year trade- and technical-oriented
community colleges.

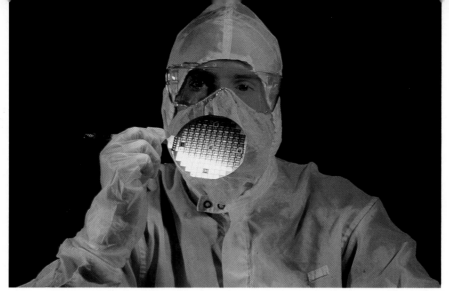

The manufacture of nonelectrical machinery, such as computers, is an important industry in Utah. This employee is holding a semiconductor wafer that will be used for producing computer chips.

Brigham Young University in Provo is a Mormon-affiliated school. It was founded in 1875 and named for the Mormon leader and first governor of the Utah Territory. With an enrollment of more than 28,000 students, it is Utah's largest university and one of the largest private universities in the world. Among its many excellent schools and departments is that of broadcast journalism. It is said that more graduates of Brigham Young University anchor the nation's evening television news broadcasts than graduates of any other college of broadcast journalism in the United States. Westminster College in Salt Lake City is a small liberal arts institution.

MANUFACTURING AND TECHNOLOGY

Manufacturing, a vital part of Utah's economy, represents about 16 percent of the gross state product. Nearly 100,000 people are employed in Utah's factories. Rocket engines for the space shuttle are made at the huge Morton Thiokol plant near Brigham City. Parts for the Pershing and MX missiles are produced at another large plant in Magna. Stouffers Foods, McDonnell Douglas, Western Gear, and Kimberly-Clark are among the state's other large employers.

In recent years, Utah has seen a mushrooming of high-technology electronic and computer companies. Some of these companies have experienced astonishing success. An example is the Word Perfect Corporation of Orem, publishers of a popular word-processing program for personal computers. Word Perfect began operation in 1979 with only its two founders as employees. Nine years later, the company employed more than a thousand people, and annual sales had ballooned to an impressive $100 million.

About 130,000 Utahans are employed in service jobs; that is, they provide services to others. Truck drivers and airplane pilots, nurses and waitresses, air-conditioner repairmen and university professors all provide services. Sears, American Express, and Fidelity Investments are among the state's largest private employers.

No one who has ever visited Utah will be surprised to learn that tourism also is a major service industry. Utah's scenic beauty is unsurpassed anywhere. Winter brings to Utah's mountains the dry, powdery snow that is best for fast and exciting skiing. Ski resorts in the Wasatch Mountains boast that it is the "greatest snow on earth." Thousands of visitors come to Salt Lake City and Temple Square to explore Utah's Mormon heritage. Since 1981, tourism has been a billion-dollar-a-year industry.

AGRICULTURE

While only a bare 3 percent of Utah's people are engaged in agriculture, farming still plays a key role in the state's economy. In 1986, cattle raised in Utah brought more than $300 million to the state. Sheep brought another $34 million, and poultry production topped $4 million. Among field crops, hay was the

most valuable, followed by barley, corn, winter wheat, and
potatoes. Apples, cherries, peaches, pears, and apricots are among
the fruits produced in Utah.

MINING AND NATURAL RESOURCES

More than two hundred different minerals have been found in
Utah. In terms of economic value, the most important minerals
produced are crude oil, natural gas, copper, and coal.

Oil production began on a large scale in 1948, and by the early
1980s had reached about 1 percent of the total United States
production. In addition to liquid petroleum, which is pumped
directly from the ground, Utah is extremely rich in oil shale, a
fine-grained rock that yields oil. Some mining engineers believe
that Utah's oil shale could yield an impressive 320 billion barrels
of oil. The technology to extract oil from the rock efficiently and
economically, however, is yet to be developed.

The Union Pacific Railroad Station in Salt Lake City was built in 1908.

Mining, which has played such an important role in Utah's history, has declined in importance in recent years. Small mines throughout the state have shut down, and for a while the future of the world's largest open-pit copper mine, which is located in Bingham Canyon, was very bleak. As world copper prices declined and labor costs increased, the colossal mine was closed. Many people thought it would never open again. But following a $400-million modernization program, the mine reopened in 1988.

TRANSPORTATION AND COMMUNICATION

Since the completion of the first transcontinental railroad at Promontory Summit in 1869, railroads have played a vital role in Utah's economy. Today, freight and passenger service is provided by ten railroads running on more than 3,000 miles (4,828 kilometers) of track. More than 25 million tons (22.7 metric tons) of freight is carried annually.

Interstate 80, sometimes called the "main road of America," passes through Salt Lake City as it wends its way from coast to

Mormon-owned
KSL-TV in
Salt Lake City
is one of
Utah's eight
television
stations.

coast. Interstate 15 crosses the state north to south from the Idaho border to St. George. In all, Utah has more than 48,000 miles (77,246 kilometers) of roads.

Salt Lake City International Airport, the state's largest airport, is a hub for Delta Air Lines. This means that it is a place where air passengers can transfer from one plane to another. Because it is also an international airport complete with customs service, Utah products can be shipped directly to anyplace in the world.

The oldest newspaper in Utah is the *Deseret News,* which was founded by the Mormon church in 1850. Today, it is second in circulation only to the *Salt Lake Tribune.* Other large dailies in Utah include the *Ogden Standard Examiner,* the Provo *Daily Herald,* and the *Logan Herald Journal.* Utah has forty-one AM radio stations and forty-seven FM radio stations. Utah's KSL Radio began broadcasting in 1922, and is one of the nation's oldest radio stations. Utah native Philo Farnsworth pioneered television in America. Utah's first television station began broadcasting in 1948, and today the state has five commercial and three educational television stations.

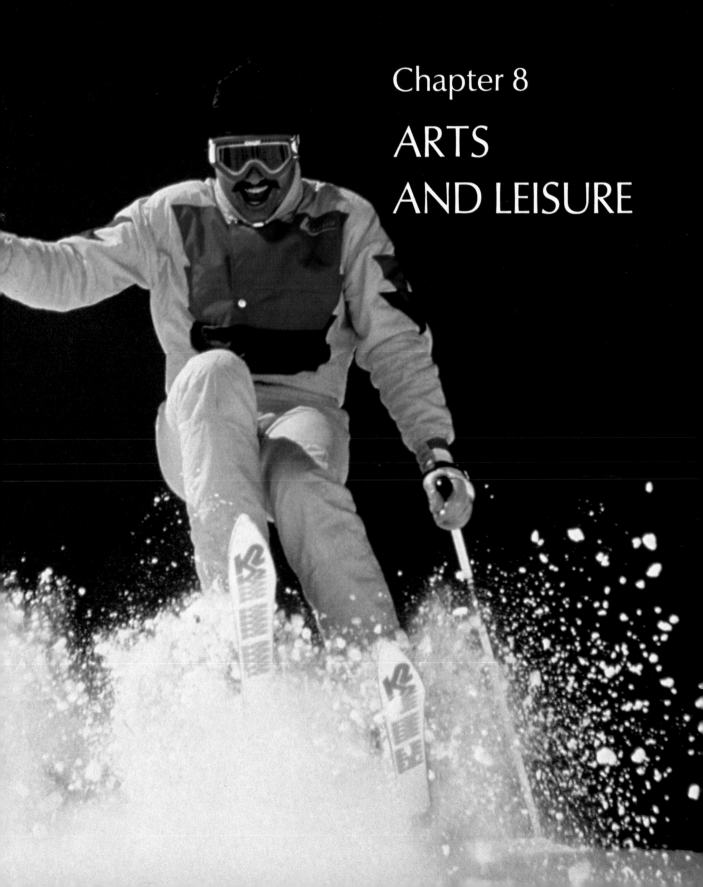

Chapter 8

ARTS AND LEISURE

ARTS AND LEISURE

LITERATURE

Brave and hardy explorers were the first literary men in Utah. The *Domínguez-Escalante Journal* and the personal observations of such mountain men as Jim Beckwourth, Jedediah Strong Smith, and Peter Skene Ogden are among the earliest literature about Utah. The journals of such government explorers as John C. Frémont and John W. Powell contained scientific detail mingled with healthy doses of sheer adventure. Later, the Mormon pioneers' incredible feat of creating green oases in a hostile land, as well as their "peculiar" institution of polygamy, drew writers like a magnet.

Mark Twain visited Salt Lake City in 1861 and included humorous, sometimes scathing, remarks on Mormon life in his book *Roughing It*. Sir Richard F. Burton, England's most famous world traveler of the time, took a more moderate view of what he called the *City of the Saints*. In 1887, Arthur Conan Doyle used Salt Lake City as a locale for the Sherlock Holmes adventure *A Study in Scarlet*.

Members of the Church of Latter-day Saints kept careful records of church history and encouraged all Mormon pioneers to keep diaries and journals. Contemporary historians indebted to this wealth of firsthand documents include Leonard J. Arrington, author of the economic history *Great Basin Kingdom*, and LeRoy

Hafen, son of a handcart emigrant, who researched many themes in Mormon and western history. Juanita Brooks of St. George used early pioneer records for her book *Mountain Meadows Massacre* and her biographies of church leaders.

Authors of western adventure novels discovered Utah in the first half of the twentieth century. A trip to the Badlands around Green River resulted in one of Zane Grey's most popular western novels, *Robber's Roost*. Frank Chester Robertson wrote some 150 books and thousands of tales about the West and westerners from his Springville home. Cowboy-author Paul Wellman's childhood in Vernal inspired such novels as *Death on the Prairie* and *Glory, God and Gold*.

Utah's most famous literary figure was Ogden-born Bernard De Voto. He won national acclaim for his regular contributions to *Harpers Magazine* and *Saturday Review* from the 1930s to the 1950s. De Voto received the 1948 Pulitzer Prize in history for his historical narrative *Across the Wide Missouri*. Another Pulitzer Prizewinner, Wallace Stegner, taught at the University of Utah in the 1930s. He drew on his Utah experience to write a stirring account of the long trek to Utah, *The Gathering of Zion*, in 1964, and a biography of De Voto in 1974. Utah's historical novelists continue to find Mormon life fascinating. *The Giant Joshua*, by Maurine Whipple, is set in a nineteenth-century Mormon village. Virginia Sorenson's *A Little Lower than the Angels* describes a woman convert caught in a plural marriage. Samuel W. Taylor incorporates some family history in his 1971 tale *Nightfall at Nauvoo*.

Utah's best-known Mormon poet was pioneer Eliza R. Snow. About a dozen of her religious poems are now standard Mormon hymns. Phyllis McGinley, whose humorous light verse earned her the 1961 Pulitzer Prize in poetry, spent her adolescence and

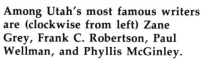

Among Utah's most famous writers are (clockwise from left) Zane Grey, Frank C. Robertson, Paul Wellman, and Phyllis McGinley.

college years in Utah. Since the 1970s, the League of Utah Writers and the Utah State Poetry Society have brought wider recognition to such Utah poets as Brewster Ghiselin and May Swenson.

THE FINE ARTS

Utah's earliest artisans were the Native Americans whose rock paintings range from crude scrawls to the huge, elaborate mural in Horseshoe (Barrier) Canyon. Modern Navajo silver and woven crafts are treasured as high art by collectors around the world.

Mormon artists arrived with the first pioneers. Daniel A. Weggeland opened the first art school in the West in 1863. Because his payment for a painting or an art lesson was sometimes only a sack of onions or a pair of hand-knitted socks, however, the school was forced to close a few months after it opened. Until 1899, Utah artists had no place to exhibit their

Modern Navajo silver and woven crafts are treasured by collectors around the world.

works and could find few paying customers. In that year, artist and state legislator Alice Merrill Horne sponsored a bill that provided for annual art exhibits; first prize would be a cash sale to the state. Because of this program, Utah became the first state in the nation with its own art collection.

The Mormon church sponsored landscape artist John Hafen's 1890 study-tour of European art. When he returned, he was commissioned to paint murals in the Salt Lake Temple. Other Utah artists in Europe at the turn of the century were Mary Teasdale and James T. Harwood. Both returned to Utah to teach future generations of artists. Brigham Young University began its annual Mormon Festival of Arts in 1968 to encourage young artists. By the 1980s, Salt Lake City, St. George, and Park City all held major annual art fairs. With opportunities to exhibit and sell their works, contemporary artists such as V. Douglas Snow, Utah's first major abstract painter, are gaining national prominence.

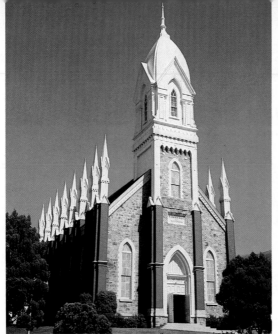 

Many of the architecturally interesting buildings of Utah are Latter-day Saint temples and tabernacles. Two of these are Box Elder Tabernacle (left), in Brigham City, and the St. George Tabernacle (right), which was built of hand-cut, native red sandstone.

Salt Lake City treasures the artistry of Utah sculptor Cyrus E. Dallin. Although he is best known for his Indian sculptures, his works also include the statue of the Angel Moroni on top of the Mormon Temple and the statue of Brigham Young in Salt Lake City. Mahonri Young was commissioned by the state to sculpt a likeness of his grandfather, Brigham Young, which now stands in the Capitol Rotunda in Washington, D.C. Young also created Utah's soaring *Sea Gull* monument and its historical *This is the Place* monument.

Architecture in Utah ranges from the awesome Anasazi ruins at Hovenweep National Monument to modern glass-and-stone buildings in the heart of Salt Lake City. Most of contemporary Utah, however, is dominated by the Latter-day Saint temples and tabernacles of Mormon architects. The St. George Tabernacle, built of hand-cut, native red sandstone, is thought by many to be the most beautiful building in the state. The Mormon Temple in Salt Lake City, built by pioneer architect Truman O. Angell, symbolizes Utah to most of the world. The nearby Salt Lake Tabernacle was constructed entirely without nails.

THE PERFORMING ARTS

When the Salt Lake Theater opened in 1862, it offered the finest drama in the Rocky Mountains. Utah's best-known actress, Maude Adams, got her start there in 1906 before going on to Broadway and *Peter Pan*, the role that made her famous. Live theater declined as the nation fell in love with motion pictures, and the Salt Lake Theater was razed in 1928. In recent years, community and college theater groups once again draw packed houses. The annual Utah Shakespearean Festival at Cedar City's Southern Utah State College draws large audiences, as do performances at the University of Utah's Pioneer Memorial Theater, a replica of the famous Salt Lake Theater.

Dance has a long tradition in Utah. Two ancient Ute dances are enacted each year. The Sun Dance is a solemn religious ritual. In contrast, the Ouray Bear Dance is a courting dance. In pioneer times, Mormons forgot hard work and hard times in the excitement of a polka, mazurka, or Virginia reel. They delighted in naming one dance the Polygamy Dance or the Brigham Young Dance because it required each man to dance with two women.

Utah became a leading center of dance in the nation after World War II, when its Ballet West became internationally famous. The colorful, joyful dancing of Brigham Young University's International Folk Dancers, Virginia Tanner's Children's Dance Theatre, and the Ririe-Woodbury Dance Company and Repertory Dance Theatre enrich the state's cultural life.

Music, like dance, helped lighten pioneer life. William Pitt's brass band crossed the plains with the first Mormon caravans. Even tiny settlements often had at least a fiddle or a dulcimer to liven up dances and get-togethers. Early in the twentieth century, Utah produced some gifted individual musicians. Emma Lucy

The Mormon Tabernacle Choir is one of the world's best-known musical groups.

Gates Bowen, granddaughter of Brigham Young, became Utah's first internationally famous opera star. Composer Leroy Robertson won a national music award in 1947 for his *Trilogy*. By midcentury, Utah concert pianist Grant Johannesen had achieved a distinguished international career.

Utah's best-known musical groups are the Mormon Tabernacle Choir and the Utah Symphony Orchestra. The choir won worldwide recognition with weekly radio broadcasts beginning in 1929, and for numerous recordings made with the Philadelphia and Utah Symphony orchestras. The success of the Utah Symphony Orchestra is largely due to the artistry of Maurice Abravanel, who became musical director in 1947. By the 1960s, he had led the orchestra to recording contracts and world tours. Joseph Silverstein, who is the current musical director of the orchestra, continues the Abravanel tradition of excellence.

Monument Valley has been the spectacular setting for dozens of western movies.

UTAH ON FILM

Utah has been attracting photographers since the 1850s. In 1869, Charles Savage captured the drama of the last linkup in the transcontinental railroad at Promontory Summit. His "golden spike" photo has been reproduced in countless history books ever since. Dorothea Lange recorded the Great Depression of the 1930s with haunting images of poverty and despair among Utah mining and farming families.

From silent films in the 1910s to science-fiction thrillers in the 1980s, Utah has been a favored background for some three hundred motion pictures. Director John Ford used Utah's Monument Valley as the backdrop for the western movie classic *Stagecoach*. John Wayne became a Hollywood legend after his first starring role in a western movie shot in Utah, and for the next forty years, Ford and other directors featured Wayne riding and shooting his way across Utah's deserts, canyons, and mountains. Paul Newman and Robert Redford were memorable as *Butch Cassidy and the Sundance Kid* in the 1969 classic. Utah also provided the spectacular scenery for the James Bond epic *Octopussy*, Biblical tales such as *The Ten Commandments*, and such science-fiction classics as *The Planet of the Apes* and *2001: A Space Odyssey*.

Television discovered Utah as the ideal setting for such 1970s series as "Grizzly Adams," "The Six Million Dollar Man," and "Gunsmoke." In the 1980s, Utah hosted the series "Airwolf" and several Donny and Marie Osmond specials.

SPORTS

The National Basketball Association Utah Jazz, formerly a New Orleans team, is Utah's major professional sports team. For the first few years in Salt Lake City, the Jazz were anything but jazzy. Under the tutelage of their coach, Frank Layden, and the brilliant play of forward Karl Malone, guard John Stockton, and center Mark Eaton, however, they improved enough to win national respect as a top contender in the NBA's Western Conference.

The University of Utah and Utah State University attract sellout crowds to their home football games. But for college football fans all over the nation, Utah football means Brigham Young University, and Brigham Young means an exciting passing game. Virgil Carter, Gifford Neilson, Jim McMahon, and Steve Young—a descendant of Brigham Young—have one thing in common. All were BYU quarterbacks who went on to success in the National Football League. In fact, it was the cocky McMahon who led the Chicago Bears to the Super Bowl Championship in 1985.

Skiing at Snowbird and white-water kayaking on the Green River are among Utah's most popular sports.

Auto racing might be a bigger sport in some places than it is in Utah, but nowhere is it faster. Bonneville Salt Flats is a salty desert as smooth and flat as the top of a pool table. In 1910, Barney Oldfield sped across the salt flats at an exciting 131.7 miles (212 kilometers) per hour. Seventy-three years later, in 1983, British driver Richard Noble roared across the same stretch of ground in a jet-powered streamliner at an astonishing 633 miles (1,019 kilometers) per hour.

For the outdoor sportsman, Utah is a year-round wonderland. In the spring, the state's vast, arid canyonlands are best explored before the hot summer sun makes hiking, and even driving, a demanding feat. In the summer, white-water rafting along the Green and Colorado rivers is among the nation's most exciting. In autumn, foliage turns a thousand shades of red and gold, and the smell of campfire smoke is in the air. Utah's fabulous snow, of course, is perfect for winter sports. In fact, any time of year is the right time to experience Utah's unique beauty and diversity.

Chapter 9

HIGHLIGHTS OF
THE BEEHIVE STATE

HIGHLIGHTS OF THE BEEHIVE STATE

My travels have taken me often, and always by car,
across the fabulous landscape of Utah. It is awesomely
beautiful. I say to myself as I gaze about me,
"It must take courage to live in such beauty."
—Pearl Buck, world traveler and Nobel Prizewinning novelist

THE GREAT BASIN

The Great Basin covers the western third of Utah. People and towns are few and far between in this region of dry valleys and low mountain ranges. Its most prominent feature is the Great Salt Lake, in the northwest. Human beings have mined the lake's salt deposits for centuries, and salt mining continues today. Huge flocks of water birds live on wetlands surrounding the lake.

The lake is a playground for nearby Salt Lake City. Bathers bob in its salty waters, and whenever the lake level permits, sailboats skim its surface. Flooding in 1983 and continued high water levels (caused by more precipitation than evaporation) closed down large areas of the lakeshore to recreational use in the late 1980s.

At Golden Spike National Historic Site, north of the lake, railroad fanciers and tourists may view working replicas of old-time steam locomotives and an annual reenactment of the final linkup of the first transcontinental railway, which was completed in 1869.

Nearby Corinne was once a rip-roaring Gentile town of two thousand railroad builders and miners where a $2 divorce "slot

Little Sahara Recreation Area has thousands of acres of shifting sand dunes.

machine" created many an ex-wife, and nightly saloon brawls created many a widow. Corinne today is home to only about six hundred people, but its railroad village museum and old railroad station help capture the excitement of the past.

West and south of the lake, United States military installations and testing ranges occupy thousands of acres of desert land. Tooele, with a population of more than fourteen thousand, is the largest city in Tooele County, south of the lake. Its major industry is the Tooele Army Depot, in existence since World War II days.

Near Wendover, at Danger Cave State Park, excavations have uncovered evidence of Desert Culture people dating back twelve thousand years. The hardships of desert life are evident at Little Sahara Recreation Area in eastern Juab County. Though its 20,000 acres (8,094 hectares) of shifting sand dunes do not seem capable of supporting any living thing, a careful observer can detect insects and small wildlife.

The Donner-Reed party's ill-fated attempt to cross the desert is remembered at Grantsville's Donner-Reed Museum, where wagon-train artifacts are on display. Old-timers claim it still is possible to find traces of caravans that passed through a hundred years ago. Look for an unnaturally straight line of boulders—pioneers had to move them off the trail. Look for the faint marks made by metal wheels scraping against stones.

Interstate 80 crosses the Great Basin south of the Great Salt Lake. It passes the Bonneville Salt Flats International Speedway—the fastest automobile raceway in the world—where test drivers have reached incredible speeds. In contrast, the old Pony Express Trail that threads through southern Tooele and northern Juab counties is impassable for long stretches for anything but a four-wheel drive vehicle.

Farther south, in Millard County, is sagebrush country, where ranching and dry farming are the main occupations. Ranchers estimate that it takes a minimum of 50 acres (20 hectares) to provide a single cow with adequate grazing. Homes are far apart and communities tend to be small. Millard County's largest town is Delta, with a population of 1,930. A marker in Delta City Park reminds visitors that the World War II Japanese relocation camp Topaz was located in the county.

SALT LAKE CITY

Salt Lake City is Utah's capital and largest city. It is tucked between the glistening Great Salt Lake on the northwest and the soaring peaks of the Wasatch and Oquirrh mountains on the east and southwest.

A visitor driving westward on Interstate Highway 80 crosses the Wasatch Mountains south of Emigration Canyon, the route of

This is the Place monument, designed by sculptor Mahonri Young, pays tribute to the early Mormon pioneers as well as those who preceded them in the Salt Lake Valley.

the pioneers. At the mouth of the canyon, the mountains part to present the first, breathtaking view of the whole valley. *This is the Place* monument at the mouth of Emigration Canyon pays tribute to Brigham Young's gallant party and to those who came before— the Spanish explorers, the mountain men, and the ill-fated Donner-Reed wagon train.

Salt Lake City's wide, tree-lined streets are a heritage of the bold plans of Mormon leaders Joseph Smith and Brigham Young. Among the buildings on Temple Square are the Mormon Temple and the Mormon Tabernacle. It took forty years to build the many-spired, gray granite temple. The domed Salt Lake Tabernacle is world famous for weekly radio broadcasts featuring its 11,000-pipe organ and nearly 400-member choir. Also at the square is the *Sea Gull* monument honoring the state bird.

It took forty years to build Salt Lake City's many-spired, gray granite Mormon Temple, the building that gave Temple Square its name.

Salt Lake City is a graceful blend of the past and the present, Mormon and Gentile. Trolley Square once garaged the city's electric trolley cars. Today it has been converted to a multilevel complex of specialty restaurants, shops, and night spots. A statue of revered church leader Brigham Young overlooks the bustling financial district. The city's tallest building is the new Church of Jesus Christ of Latter-day Saints Office Building, which has an observation deck on the twenty-sixth floor. Two historic structures, Lion House and Beehive House, have been restored. The houses, once used as Brigham Young's offices and official residence, are just a short distance away from the massive and modern Salt Palace, a convention center and new home for Utah's professional sports teams.

On Capitol Hill, north of downtown, the copper-domed state capitol symbolizes another city, the administrative heart of Utah.

Two of Salt Lake City's historic buildings are the Governor's Mansion (left) and Devereaux House (right), the first mansion built in the city.

The Governor's Mansion was once the lavish home of millionaire miner, publisher, and anti-Mormon Thomas Kearns. The nearby "Marmalade District" contains many of Salt Lake City's oldest homes, some dating from the 1850s.

The nationally renowned Utah Symphony Orchestra and the Ballet West dance company perform to Salt Lake City crowds. There is an opera company and several professional theater groups. The city has fifty-four parks, a variety of history and art museums, and the world's largest collection of genealogical books and records.

The University of Utah was founded at Salt Lake City in 1850 as the University of Deseret. By the late 1980s, it had grown to include more than a hundred permanent buildings. The world's first operation implanting an artificial heart in a human being was performed at the university's medical center.

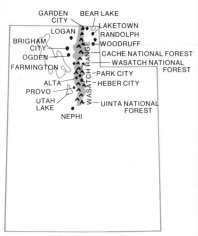

Beautiful Bear Lake is on the Utah-Idaho border.

ALONG THE WASATCH FRONT

The rugged Wasatch Mountains run north-south through central Utah for 150 miles (241 kilometers) from the Utah-Idaho border to Mount Nebo, at Nephi. Utah's oldest and largest cities are nestled along the western front of the Wasatch. The Wasatch-Cache and Uinta national forests cloak the mountains with abundant wildflowers, summer greenery, and a magnificent display of fall color. Heavy snows blanket the peaks in the winter.

In the far north, the Rich County towns of Woodruff and Randolph are Utah's cold spots, with winter temperatures dipping well below 0 degrees Fahrenheit (minus 17.7 degrees Celsius). Cache and Rich counties are called "Bridgerland," because Jim Bridger and other fur trappers frequented beautiful, turquoise-blue Bear Lake, on the Utah-Idaho border. Garden City and Laketown are modern resorts frequented by visitors who enjoy fishing through the winter ice for the small Bonneville cisco, found only in Bear Lake.

The summit of Logan Canyon offers a panoramic view of Bear Lake and a 30-mile (48-kilometer) scenic drive westward to Logan, the dairying and cheese-making center of the north. Logan's Mormon Temple overlooks the city and is visible for miles around. Brigham Young himself selected the site. Center Street, with its many fine mansions and one of Utah's most interesting old railroad stations, is a national historic district. Utah State University at Logan has an enrollment of about 11,000 students and an international reputation for excellence in such fields as space technology, engineering, and agriculture.

Brigham City, in Box Elder County, is famous for peaches and other orchard crops. From July to September, so many fruit stands line Highway 89 south of the city that it is called "Fruitway." Morton Thiokol, the giant rocket-industry manufacturer, is the area's major employer.

Fur trapper Peter Skene Ogden gave his name to Utah's second-largest city. Mormons settled Ogden in 1850, buying out the fort and trading center of Miles Goodyear, another fur trapper. The Goodyear home is Utah's oldest pioneer dwelling. Modern Ogden is the railroad center for the intermountain area. The Weber State College student body increases Ogden's population by 11,000 during the school year.

Bountiful and Farmington were settled in 1847, the same year as Salt Lake City, but just to the north of it. Farmington's Rock Chapel is a famous landmark. Built in 1861-63 by 160 families, it is a testimony to the Mormon pioneer traits of cooperation and public spirit.

South of Salt Lake City lies Utah Valley, famous for its cherry crop and the state's richest agricultural and fruit-producing region. Its Utah Lake is the largest natural freshwater lake in the West.

Park City is a trendy tourist town known for its ski slopes, historic buildings, artisan community, and summer theater.

Provo, named for mountain man Etienne Provost, was founded two years after Salt Lake City. Modern Provo, Utah's third-largest city, is a commercial and industrial center. Its Brigham Young University is one of the world's largest private universities. The university, along with Provo and its sister city, Orem, support a burgeoning new computer-software industry.

Historic mining and railroad towns dot the mountains between Salt Lake City and Orem-Provo. The mineral-rich Oquirrh Mountains, called "Shining Mountains" by the Indians, are a parallel spur of the Wasatch below the Great Salt Lake. The Bingham Copper Mine in Bingham Canyon still lures tourists with its observation deck that overlooks the "biggest man-made hole in the world."

Across the Wasatch to the east, Park City silver mines once made many Utahans millionaires. When the ore veins ran out, Park City was well on its way to becoming a ghost town—until skiers discovered it. Today, Park City is a trendy tourist town, known equally for ski slopes, historic buildings, an artisan community, a summer theater, and its annual Shakespeare

The "Heber Creeper" train makes regular scenic tours through Heber Valley and Provo Canyon.

festival. The former mining towns of Brighton and Alta also are popular winter-sport resorts. Movie star Robert Redford's Sundance Resort offers summer theater in addition to winter sports.

A stop at Heber is a must for its railroad museum and a ride on the "Heber Creeper," a steam engine that threads through forested Heber Valley and Provo Canyon to Bridal Veil Falls. An aerial tramway rises 1,753 feet (534 meters) above the floor of Provo Canyon, offering a breathtaking view of the falls.

Timpanogos Cave National Monument is about 15 miles (24 kilometers) northeast of Provo. It is reached by a strenuous 1.5-mile (2.4-kilometer) hike leading 1,065 feet (325 meters) straight up through spectacular scenery. Three interconnected limestone caverns sparkle with hundreds of beautifully colored stalagmites and stalactites. Seeping water slowly but continuously builds new "live" dripstones.

Mount Nebo marks the southern end of the Wasatch. From here, a series of lower ranges and plateaus curve southwestward to form the rim of the Great Basin.

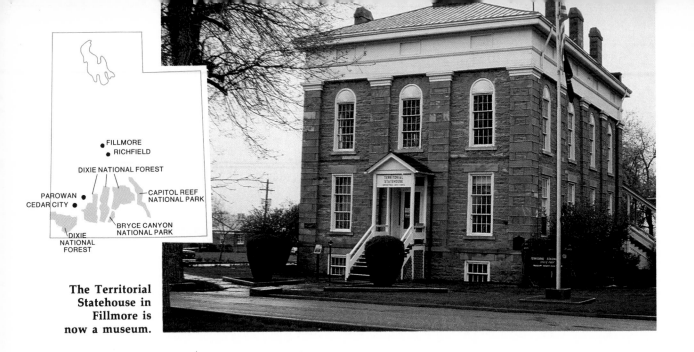

The map shows locations in southwestern Utah:

FILLMORE
RICHFIELD
DIXIE NATIONAL FOREST
PAROWAN
CEDAR CITY
CAPITOL REEF NATIONAL PARK
BRYCE CANYON NATIONAL PARK
DIXIE NATIONAL FOREST

The Territorial Statehouse in Fillmore is now a museum.

THE SOUTHWEST

When Utah Territory was created in 1850, Brigham Young established a new settlement to be the site of the territorial capital. He named it Fillmore for Millard Fillmore, who was then president of the United States. The main population centers were farther north, however, and the territorial government soon moved to Salt Lake City. The original statehouse is now a museum featuring Indian and pioneer relics and a collection of paintings by Utah artists.

Richfield, southeast of Fillmore in Sevier County, is the agricultural and commercial center of the area. South of Richfield, Big Rock Candy Mountain lives up to part of its name. It is the same color as a lemon-drop candy, but only in Burl Ives's popular song is it a big mountain. Nearby Fremont Indian State Park is an interpretative center and museum for the prehistoric Indian culture that developed in Utah.

The earliest Mormon settlements in southern Utah were

Parowan and Cedar City, founded in 1851 to develop local iron
mines. Unusual pioneer architecture, from log cabins to stone
houses, attracts visitors to Beaver, settled in 1856.

Cedar City today is the home of Southern Utah State College
and its annual Utah Shakespeare Festival. It also is the gateway to
some of southwestern Utah's most magnificent scenery. East of
Cedar City, on a high, cool plateau within the Dixie National
Forest, is Cedar Breaks National Monument, a giant natural
amphitheater, or basin, with massive, furrowed walls. The Indians
knew it as "circle of painted cliffs." Minerals in the rock give the
effect of an artist's easel—hot, blazing reds, golds, oranges, and
blinding white in midday light, turning to cool purples and blues
at dusk.

Bryce Canyon National Park is part of the same geologic
formation as Cedar Breaks. But Bryce is much larger, a series of
fourteen giant amphitheaters. The walls and spires at Bryce are
carved into delicate, almost lacy shapes, painted in soft, pastel
colors on the rocks.

The Castle
is one of
the fantastic
sandstone
formations
in Capitol
Reef National
Park.

Highway 12 links Bryce Canyon to Capitol Reef National Park. The section of highway between Boulder and Torrey is one of the most scenic routes in the nation. Capitol Reef, 65 miles (105 kilometers) long, is a red sandstone cliff with "forests" of petrified wood, Indian ruins and rock art, and the remnants of a pioneer Mormon village where so many fruit trees were planted that it took the name Fruita. The park was named for Capitol Dome, a towering, red rock outcrop whose general shape and white sandstone capping were said to resemble the Capitol in Washington, D.C.

The Jacob
Hamblin home
in Santa
Clara

UTAH'S DIXIE

Snow is rare, winters are mild, and summers are hot in the southwestern corner of the state. Because the distinctive climate reminded the Mormons of the southern United States, Brigham Young encouraged its settlers to try to grow cotton and grapes. Young's winter home at St. George is preserved as a museum with period furnishings. St. George's gleaming white Mormon Temple and red sandstone tabernacle are distinctive landmarks.

Jacob Hamblin, Mormon missionary to the Indians, helped settle Santa Clara. Some 30 miles (48 kilometers) away, a simple marker reminds travelers along State Highway 18 of the infamous Mountain Meadows Massacre in which both Hamblin and John D. Lee were involved.

Over tens of thousands of years, the Virgin River cut a deep, narrow canyon through what is now Zion National Park. Its brilliantly colored, towering walls are decorated with waterfalls and hanging gardens and studded with fossilized shells, fish, and plants. Prehistoric Indian ruins perch high up in the cliffs. Here

101

and there, canyon walls open up into alcoves and amphitheaters where visitors imagine statues, cathedrals, and thrones in the fantastic rock formations.

THE SOUTHEAST

The Colorado River cuts through southeastern Utah's fabulous canyonlands. The world's second-largest man-made reservoir, 200-mile- (322-kilometer-) long Lake Powell, runs through the Glen Canyon National Recreation Area. Boaters on the lake can explore hundreds of side canyons lined with Anasazi Indian ruins and rock art.

Soaring above Lake Powell's southeastern shoreline is Rainbow Bridge, the world's largest natural bridge. A ribbon hewn of sandstone, it arches to a height of 290 feet (88 meters), with a span of 270 feet (82 meters). The Navajos revere it as a sacred place.

Rainbow Bridge lies within the huge Navajo Indian Reservation that stretches across southern Lake Powell to Four Corners, where the borders of Utah, Colorado, Arizona, and New Mexico meet. The classic 1939 film *Stagecoach* was filmed in the reservation's Monument Valley, a severely beautiful passage of red desert bordered by high buttes and towers.

The San Juan River, which forms part of the northern boundary of the Navajo Reservation, has carved a spectacular chasm near Mexican Hat. It is called the Goosenecks of the San Juan.

Along the 100-mile (161-kilometer) Trail of the Ancients that loops between Mexican Hat and Blanding are Anasazi ruins and countless examples of Indian rock art. Side trips lead to Hovenweep National Monument's prehistoric ruins and to Natural Bridges National Monument.

GREEN RIVER

ARCHES
NATIONAL PARK

CANYONLANDS
NATIONAL PARK

• MOAB

COLORADO
RIVER

NATURAL BRIDGES NATIONAL
MONUMENT

GLEN CANYON
NATIONAL
RECREATION AREA

• MONTICELLO

BLANDING

HOVENNEEP
NATIONAL
MONUMENT

SAN JUAN RIVER

LAKE POWELL

MEXICAN HAT

NAVAJO INDIAN
RESERVATION

**Glen Canyon National
Recreation Area is
the location of such
varied natural scenery
as Rainbow Bridge
(left), the world's
largest natural
bridge, and the
sculpted dunes near
Hog Spring (below).**

The Island in the Sky region offers a spectacular panoramic view of Canyonlands National Park and its two mighty rivers, the Green and Colorado.

Blanding is the gateway to the roadless Dark Canyon Primitive Area, a hiker's wilderness paradise. The flat surface of Newspaper Rock, near Monticello, displays at least three distinct periods of Native American rock art.

Monticello and Moab enjoyed short-lived uranium booms after World War II. Moab long has been a filming center for motion pictures and television specials. Tourists know the two towns best as entrances to Canyonlands National Park.

There is no more glorious scenery in the world than Canyonlands. At nearly 340,000 acres (137,595 hectares), it is Utah's largest national park. Because it has no paved roads, only primitive camping areas, and limited water supplies, it is best experienced by hiking, jeeping, and rafting.

The Colorado and Green rivers slice through the park, cutting it up into three districts. Island in the Sky, 2,000 feet (610 meters) above the park floor, offers visitors the best panoramic view of Canyonlands and its two mighty rivers. Narrow, clustered spires of white-banded sandstones give The Needles its name. Tall

Delicate Arch is probably the best known of the more than two hundred arches within the boundaries of Utah's Arches National Park.

standing rocks and colorful sandstone fins grace the twisting, tortuous canyons of The Maze, the most remote and seldom-visited part of Canyonlands.

Dead Horse Point, on the road to Moab, offers a spectacular view down to the Colorado River and back across into Canyonlands. Legend has it that the promontory got its name because a herd of wild mustangs lost their way here and died of thirst only half a mile (four-fifths of a kilometer) away—straight down—from the river.

The land north of Moab is deceptively level, punctuated by a few red-rock reefs and canyons. But hidden in its canyons is the world's largest concentration of sandstone arches. Cowboys ranging the canyons in the 1920s were amazed to learn that an Arches National Monument was proposed. "Nothin' out there," they said, "jest a lot of holes in rocks." High and solitary Delicate Arch, with its window to the distant La Sal Mountains, was called "the schoolmarm's britches" by the cowboys. Double Arch was known as "jughandles."

THE NORTHEAST

Dinosaurs, Indians, Spanish priests, cowboys, and outlaws have contributed to the history and flavor of northeastern Utah. The state's largest Indian reservation is the Uintah and Ouray Reservation in the Uinta Basin and its Hill Creek Extension along the Green River on the Colorado Plateau. Fort Duchesne, which in the 1880s housed two companies of black infantrymen, who were known as "Buffalo Soldiers," today is headquarters for the reservation.

Butch Cassidy and his Wild Bunch roamed both sides of the Green River. A posse thought they had killed Cassidy near Price City in 1898, but when a throng came to view the body, one man at the back kept chuckling. When the body was later identified as another outlaw, everyone realized that the man had been Cassidy himself. A tombstone in Price Cemetery commemorates the event.

The Domínguez-Escalante expedition entered Utah at Jensen, southeast of Vernal. Highway 40 parallels much of their trail through present-day Jensen, Myton, Roosevelt, and Duchesne.

Vernal is famous for its "mail-order" bank. In 1919, it cost twice as much to bring bricks in by freight as it did to mail them parcel post. So Vernal residents began ordering bricks by mail, while local ranchers and farmers took to having tools and canned goods mailed in. The federal post office soon changed its shipping rules.

When visitors to Vernal's Dinosaur Gardens and Dinosaur Museum tire of watching scientists painstakingly excavate nearby Dinosaur National Monument, they can study fossils and life-size dinosaur skeletons. The quarry has produced more skulls, bones, and complete skeletons of dinosaurs than any other site.

Manila, in northeastern Utah, got its name because it was being surveyed at the time Manila in the Philippines was captured

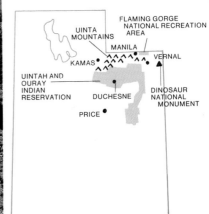

Water-skiers at Flaming Gorge Reservoir near Cart Creek Bridge

during the Spanish-American War. It is the main entrance to one of the scenic wonders of Utah and of the West—Flaming Gorge National Recreation Area on the Green River. The 91-mile- (146-kilometer-) long Flaming Gorge Reservoir is shared by Utah and Wyoming. The Red Canyon overlook offers one of Utah's most spectacular vistas.

The snow-covered, forested Uintas, Utah's highest mountains, run along the border with Wyoming. Few roads penetrate the Uintas, but Highway 150, stretching between Kamas on the west and Manila on the east, is a magnificent scenic drive. Utahans say that horseback riding and backpacking are the best ways to appreciate this wild paradise where trout all but leap right out of a thousand beautiful mountain lakes. There are almost as many campsites in the Uintas as there are tiny towns.

Utah offers something for everyone. It has warm, friendly people and fantastic yet diverse scenery. A million and a half people call the state home. More than five million visitors each year call it wonderful.

FACTS AT A GLANCE

GENERAL INFORMATION

Statehood: January 4, 1896, forty-fifth state

Origin of Name: Named for the Ute Indians, who lived there; *Eutaw* is an Indian word meaning "dwellers in the tops of the mountains"

State Capital: Salt Lake City

State Nickname: Beehive State

State Flag: Utah's state flag, adopted in 1913, consists of a blue field within which is centered the state coat of arms and the year of statehood, 1896, both enclosed in a thin gold circle. The coat of arms displays a shield, flanked with American flags and topped with an eagle. Within the shield is a beehive and the state motto, "Industry," with six arrows above, the date "1847" (the year of Mormon settlement) below, and sego lilies on either side.

State Motto: Industry

State Bird: Sea gull

State Animal: Rocky Mountain elk

State Flower: Sego lily

State Tree: Blue spruce

State Gem: Topaz

State Insect: Honeybee

State Fish: Rainbow trout

State Song: "Utah, We Love Thee," written by Evan Stephens of Salt Lake City, was adopted as the official state song February 21, 1917.

> Land of the mountains high, Utah, we love thee,
> Land of the sunny sky, Utah, we love thee!
> Far in the glorious west, throned on the mountain's crest,
> In robes of statehood dressed, Utah, we love thee!
>
> Columbia's brightest star, Utah, we love thee,
> Thy luster shines afar, Utah, we love thee!
> Bright in our banner's blue, among her sisters true
> She proudly comes to view, Utah, we love thee!
>
> Land of the Pioneers, Utah, we love thee,
> Grow with the coming years, Utah, we love thee!
> With wealth and peace in store, to fame and glory soar,
> God guarded, evermore, Utah, we love thee!

POPULATION

Population: 1,461,037, thirty-sixth among the states (1980 census)

Population Density: 17 people per sq. mi. (7 people per km²)

Population Distribution: 84 percent of the people live in cities or towns. About three-fourths of the people live in the Salt Lake City-Ogden and Provo-Orem metropolitan areas.

Salt Lake City	163,034
Provo	74,108
Ogden	64,407
Orem	52,399
Sandy City	52,210
Bountiful	32,877
West Jordan	27,315
Logan	26,844
Murray	25,750
Layton	22,862
Roy	19,694
Clearfield	17,982
Brigham City	15,596

(Population figures according to 1980 census)

Population Growth: Utah's population increased about 2,000 percent between 1847, when the Mormons arrived, and the 1890s. Most of the newcomers were converts to the Church of Jesus Christ of Latter-day Saints who came from the United States, Canada, and northern Europe. In the 1890s, non-Mormon immigrants arrived to look for work in mining, railroading, and agriculture.

The Brigham Young statue stands just outside Temple Square in the middle of Salt Lake City's Main Street.

During the twentieth century, Utah's population doubled nearly every forty years, and today it is among the fastest-growing states in the nation. The list below shows population growth in Utah since statehood in 1896:

Year	Population
1900	276,749
1920	449,396
1940	550,310
1960	890,627
1970	1,059,037
1980	1,461,037

GEOGRAPHY

Borders: States that border Utah are Idaho on the north, Wyoming on the northeast, Colorado on the east, Arizona and New Mexico on the south, and Nevada on the west.

Highest Point: Kings Peak, 13,528 ft. (4,123 m)

Lowest Point: Beaverdam Creek, near St. George, 2,000 ft. (610 m)

Greatest Distances: North to south—345 mi. (555 km)
East to west—275 mi. (442 km)

Area: 84,899 sq. mi. (219,888 km²)

Rank in Area Among the States: Eleventh

Flaming Gorge Reservoir cuts through a beautiful red-sandstone canyon.

Indian Reservations: Indian reservations occupy more than 1 million acres (.4 million hectares) of land in Utah. The largest reservation entirely within the state is the Ute Indians' Uintah and Ouray Reservation and its Hill Creek Extension in eastern Utah. The Navajo Reservation of New Mexico and Arizona juts up into Utah's San Juan County in the southeast. Smaller reservations house the Southern Paiutes and the Gosiutes in south and southwestern Utah.

Rivers: Utah's largest rivers, the Colorado and the Green, flow south and southwestward, draining the eastern half of the state. Dams and lakes created along the two rivers provide water for Utah and its neighboring states. The Jordan River, which flows north from Utah Lake, and the Bear, Provo, and Weber rivers, which arise in the Uinta Mountains and flow westward, are landlocked rivers; that is, they empty into the Great Salt Lake without reaching a sea or an ocean. The Sevier is the main river of south-central Utah; it, too, is landlocked, ending its course in the Great Basin. The Virgin River, in the southwest, flows out of the state into Nevada's Lake Mead. In the northwest, the Raft River flows into Idaho's Snake River.

Lakes: Utah's largest natural lake—and the largest natural lake west of the Mississippi River—is the Great Salt Lake. It is saltier than any sea except the Dead Sea. The Great Salt Lake's saltiness and size depend on evaporation and precipitation. It averages about 30 mi. (48 km) in width and 75 mi. (121 km) in length. The only other large natural lakes in the state are freshwater lakes: Utah Lake in north-central Utah and Bear Lake at the Utah-Idaho border. Thousands of small glacial lakes dot Utah's Wasatch and Uinta mountains. The state's largest man-made lake is Lake Powell, in the southwest. Nearly 200 mi. (322 km) long, it was formed by a dam on the Colorado River. Flaming Gorge Reservoir, on the Green River, is 90 mi. (145 km) long; it is shared by Utah and Wyoming. There are hundreds of dams and small storage lakes throughout the state.

Topography: Utah has three major topographical regions: the Basin and Range Region, the Rocky Mountains, and the Colorado Plateau. The western third of Utah lies in the Basin and Range Region. It was named the Great Basin because it is a basin, or depression, in the land without drainage to any ocean or sea. The vast expanse of the Great Basin is dry, flat land broken up by short mountain ranges. Prominent features include the Great Salt Lake in the northeast, and the Great Salt Lake, Sevier, and Escalante deserts in the west and south. Bonneville Salt Flats is sun-baked to a hard, smooth surface much of the year, and has become famous for automobile-racing trials.

Two ranges of the Rocky Mountains dominate north-central Utah. The Wasatch Range includes peaks more than 11,000 ft. (3,353 m) high. It runs north from Mount Nebo, at Nephi, to the Utah-Idaho border. Utah's major cities are concentrated along the western slope, called the Wasatch Front. The Uinta Range runs east-west along the Utah-Wyoming border from near Salt Lake City to Colorado. Its twin-domed Kings Peak is Utah's highest mountain.

About half of Utah lies within the Colorado Plateau, a series of broad uplands deeply cut through by the canyons of the Colorado and Green rivers and their tributaries. Its brilliantly colored rocks have been sculpted by wind and water erosion to create magnificent arches, bridges, and spires. The Henry, Abajo, and La Sal are the major mountain ranges of the region.

Climate: Utah's climate is generally sunny, warm, and dry, with variations according to latitude (distance from the equator) and elevation (height above sea level). Average annual precipitation (rain and snowfall) is 15 in. (38 cm) at Salt Lake City. The Great Basin and Colorado Plateau regions average less than 5 in. (13 cm), while the Wasatch and Uinta ranges may average almost 50 in. (127 cm) of precipitation each year. Temperatures at Salt Lake City range from a January average of 28° F. (-2° C) to a July average of 77° F. (25° C). Utah's "Dixie," in the southwestern corner of the state, has an almost semitropical climate. The state's

Prickly pear cactus, shown here growing in Zion National Park, is one of the more than four thousand species of wild plants found in Utah.

highest recorded temperature occurred on July 5, 1985, when thermometers in St. George registered 117° F. (47° C). The north-central mountains regularly experience Utah's coldest temperatures. Utah's lowest temperature, -50° F. (-46° C), was reached at Strawberry Tunnel on January 5, 1913, and at Woodruff on February 6, 1899.

NATURE

Trees: Forests cover about 30 percent of the state. Common trees include aspens, balsams, birches, black walnuts, blue spruces, box elders, cottonwoods, elms, firs, junipers, locusts, maples, oaks, pines, sycamores, and willows.

Wild Plants: Some 4,000 plant species, from desert to alpine, are found in Utah, including cactuses, chokecherries, creosote bushes, dogtooth violets, grasses, greasewoods, hawthorn bushes, Indian paintbrush, Joshua trees, lupines, mesquite, prickly pears, sagebrush, sego lilies, tamarisks, wild roses, wild sweet Williams, and yucca.

Animals: Antelopes, bears, beavers, bighorn sheep, bobcats, buffaloes, cougars, coyotes, desert tortoises, elks, foxes, jackrabbits, lizards, lynxes, mink, moose, mule deer, otters, porcupines, prairie dogs, squirrels, and snakes

Birds: Ducks, eagles, grouse, hawks, herons, magpies, ouzels, owls, pelicans, pheasants, quail, sea gulls, titmice, and a great variety of songbirds

Fish: Bass, Bonneville cisco, brine shrimp, carp, catfish, graylings, perch, suckers, trout, and whitefish

GOVERNMENT

The government of Utah, like that of the United States, is divided into three branches—legislative, executive, and judicial.

The legislature consists of a 29-member senate and a 75-member house of representatives. State senators serve four-year terms and state representatives serve two-year terms. The legislature decides which proposals, or bills, will become law, but before a bill becomes law it must be signed by the governor. Two-thirds of the members of the legislature can vote to override the governor's veto and make it a law even without the governor's signature. The legislature meets annually on the second Monday in January.

The executive department is headed by the governor, who is elected to a four-year term. The governor may serve any number of terms. The governor has the power to appoint many important state officials, to approve or veto (reject) proposed laws, and, in times of emergency, to call out the state militia. Other important officers in the executive department are the lieutenant governor, the attorney general, the state auditor, and the state treasurer, all of whom are elected by the people to serve four-year terms. If the governorship becomes vacant, the lieutenant governor serves as governor. Since Utah does not have a secretary of state, most of the duties of that office are performed by the lieutenant governor.

Utah's judicial branch consists of a supreme court, district courts, circuit courts, and justices of the peace. There is also a statewide system of juvenile courts. The supreme court has five members who serve staggered ten-year terms. Every two years a new justice joins the court and the justice with only two years left to serve becomes the chief justice. Members are appointed by the governor, but they must be approved by the voters in the following general election. The supreme court can declare state laws unconstitutional, and it hears appeals from the lower courts.

Number of Counties: 29

U.S. Representatives: 3

Electoral Votes: 5

Voting Qualifications: United States citizen, at least eighteen years of age, with thirty days residency

EDUCATION

The constitution of 1895, adopted just two months before statehood, called for free public schools. Today, approximately 40 percent of the state budget is spent on educating the more than 230,000 elementary students and 165,000 secondary students who attend Utah's public schools. Utah is among the national leaders in percentage of school-age children attending school, percentage of students graduating from high school, and percentage of students who go on to college.

The state's largest public university is the University of Utah at Salt Lake City, with more than 24,000 students. Other public-supported universities are Utah

State University in Logan, with 13,000 students, Weber State in Ogden, with an enrollment of 11,000, and Southern Utah State College in Cedar City, with 2,500. Two-year state colleges, scattered throughout the state, include Dixie College in St. George, the College of Eastern Utah in Price, and Snow College in Ephraim. Salt Lake City and Orem have two-year trade- and technical-oriented community colleges. Brigham Young University in Provo, with an enrollment of more than 28,000, is the state's largest university, public or private. Westminster College in Salt Lake City is a small private college.

ECONOMY AND INDUSTRY

Principal Products:
Agriculture: Dairy products, wheat, hay, sugar beets, barley, potatoes, corn, onions, dry beans, oats, truck-garden vegetables, eggs and poultry, greenhouse and nursery products, apples, peaches, cherries, pears, apricots, hogs, beef and dairy cattle, sheep, lambs, turkeys
Manufacturing: Cement, primary metals, nonelectrical machinery, fabricated metals, transportation equipment, petroleum refining, electrical machinery, printing and publishing, chemicals and allied products, furniture, food processing, lumber and wood products, computer software
Natural Resources: Petroleum, coal, natural gas, copper, gold, silver, Gilsonite (asphalt), salt, molybdenum, potassium, sand, gravel, clay, gemstones, gypsum, phosphate rock, lead, zinc, potash, beryllium, uranium, and iron

Business and Trade: Manufacturing provides about 15 percent of the total state employment and more than 17 percent of total earnings. Rocket engines for the space shuttle are made by Morton Thiokol near Brigham City. Parts for the Pershing and MX strategic missiles are produced by Hercules Aerospace at Magna. Stouffers Foods, McDonnell Douglas, Western Gear, and Kimberly-Clark are among the state's other large manufacturers.
Retail trade is conducted by more than 8,000 establishments. Another 2,500 are engaged in wholesale trade. Combined retail and wholesale trade accounts for about 23 percent of all employment. More than 130,000 persons, or 21 percent of the work force, is engaged in service industries. Tourism is one of the fastest-growing sectors of the state economy.

Communication: The oldest newspaper in Utah is the *Deseret News*, which was founded by the Mormon church in 1850. Today, it is second in circulation only to the *Salt Lake Tribune*. Other large dailies in Utah include the *Ogden Standard Examiner*, the Provo *Daily Herald*, and the *Logan Herald Journal*. Utah has 41 AM radio stations and 47 FM radio stations. Utah's KSL Radio began broadcasting in 1922, and is one of the nation's oldest radio stations. Utah's first television station began broadcasting in 1948, and today the state has 5 commercial and 3 educational television stations.

Transportation: Freight and passenger service is provided by ten railroads running on more than 3,000 mi. (4,828 km) of track. Utah railroads carry some

Old Deseret, in Pioneer Trail State Park, is a re-created pioneer town. Among the items on display is a handcart (top left) that was used by a family of Mormons who crossed the country on the Mormon Trail.

25 million tons (22.7 million metric tons) of freight annually. U.S. Interstate 80 crosses the state east to west. Interstate 15 runs north to south from the Idaho border to St. George. In all, Utah has more than 48,000 mi. (77,246 km) of roads.

Salt Lake City International Airport, a hub for Delta Air Lines, is the state's largest airport.

SOCIAL AND CULTURAL LIFE

Museums: Salt Lake City's largest art museums are the Salt Lake Art Center and the Utah Museum of Fine Arts at the University of Utah. Both feature many works by local and regional artists. The Museum of Natural History, also at the University of Utah, has many "hands-on" exhibits for children. Two important museums at Brigham Young University in Provo are the B.F. Larsen Gallery and the Monte L. Bean Life Sciences Museum. The Springville Museum of Art in Springville is highly regarded for its collection of works by Utah artists. Historical museums in Salt Lake City include the Daughters of Utah Pioneers collection and the Mormon-owned Museum of Church History and Art. Pioneer Trail State Park in Salt Lake City houses Old Deseret, a re-created pioneer town. The Man and His Bread Museum and Historical Farm near Logan feature the development of farming in early Utah. The Utah Prehistoric Museum at Price houses an extensive collection of dinosaur tracks, dinosaur skeletons, and a dinosaur egg; the nearby Emery County Museum also has many dinosaur skeletons, as does the State Natural History Museum at Vernal.

117

Libraries: Utah has had free public libraries since the 1890s. The Utah State Library Commission, established in 1957, provides assistance to approximately 50 public libraries. Salt Lake City and Ogden have the state's oldest and largest library systems. Brigham Young University, the University of Utah, and the Utah State Historical Society have extensive collections dealing with Mormon and Utah state history as well as the arts and sciences. Perhaps the most important library in the state is the Mormon Genealogical Library in Salt Lake City, which contains the world's largest collection of genealogical records.

Performing Arts: Utah's best-known musical groups are the Mormon Tabernacle Choir and the Utah Symphony Orchestra. The choir has won worldwide recognition for its numerous recordings and its weekly radio broadcasts, which began in 1929. Under the direction of Maurice Abravanel, musical director from 1947 to 1980, the Utah Symphony Orchestra won an international reputation for excellence. Joseph Silverstein, musical director since 1983, continues the tradition of excellence.

Important dance groups include the internationally famous Ballet West, Brigham Young University's International Folk Dancers, Virginia Tanner's Children's Dance Theatre, and the Ririe-Woodbury Dance Company.

Annual Utah Shakespeare festivals at Cedar City and Park City draw admiring audiences from across the country. Live drama and comedy productions are held at numerous other sites throughout the state. Dramatic performances are featured at Pioneer Memorial Theater, a replica of the famed Salt Lake Theater at the University of Utah.

Sports and Recreation: Utah's best-known professional sports team is the Utah Jazz of the National Basketball Association, which plays its home games before packed houses at the Salt Palace in Salt Lake City. Brigham Young University, the University of Utah, and Utah State University attract sellout crowds to their home football games. Weber State, in Ogden, and Brigham Young also are perennial powerhouses in basketball.

The Bonneville Speedway, 120 mi. (193 km) west of Salt Lake City, is the world's fastest speedway. Automobile test drivers speed more than 600 mi. (966 km) per hour on its sunbaked salt flats.

Rodeos are held at Oakley, Vernal, Salt Lake City, Ogden, and Santa Clara, and county fairs are held throughout the state. In recent years, skiing has become a major source of income as thousands of out-of-staters and local residents take advantage of Utah's famed snow. Today, the state has more than sixteen ski resorts, seven of which are less than an hour's drive from Salt Lake City.

Utah has five national parks, forty-eight state parks, six national monuments, two national recreation areas, and thousands of acres of national forest. More than a thousand fishable lakes and streams produce such anglers' delights as rainbow and brown trout, striped bass, walleyes, bluegills, whitefish, Bonneville cisco, and many species of sports fish. Hunters will find deer, elk, antelope, pheasants, sage grouse, and chukar partridges. Or they may apply for a once-in-a-lifetime permit to hunt buffalo, desert bighorn sheep, moose, or Rocky Mountain goats. White-water rafting on the Green and Colorado rivers is among the most exciting and spectacular in the nation. Camping, backpacking, and off-road four-wheel driving in the state's arid canyonlands are unique and rewarding experiences.

The completion of the nation's first transcontinental railroad is reenacted every year at Golden Spike National Historic Site, where working replicas of the original locomotives are on display.

Historic Sites and Landmarks:

Beaver National Historic District, in Beaver, has more than thirty preserved buildings. The Beaver County Courthouse, originally built between 1876 and 1882, was destroyed by fire and then rebuilt.

Benson Historic Grist Mill, near Tooele, was built in the 1860s. This early flour mill now offers tours to the public.

Center Street, a National Historic District in Logan, is part of the largest historic district between the Rocky Mountains and Sacramento. It features many early Utah mansions and one of the state's finest early railroad stations.

Exchange Place National Historic District, in Salt Lake City, was once the non-Mormon center of commerce.

Golden Spike National Historic Site, at Promontory, is where the golden spike completed the nation's first transcontinental railroad in 1869. Working replicas of the original locomotives are on display from May to September.

Jacob Hamblin Home, in Santa Clara, was built in the 1850s. Hamblin, a noted Mormon missionary to the Indians, was one of the earliest settlers in the area.

Miles Goodyear Home, in Ogden, is Utah's oldest private dwelling. Fur trapper Miles Goodyear originally built this simple cabin on the Ogden River in 1841. It is now situated next to the Daughters of the Utah Pioneers Museum in Ogden.

Salt Lake City and County Building, in Salt Lake City, was built between 1891 and 1894 on Washington Square, where the first group of pioneers camped in 1847. A $30-million renovation was completed in April 1989.

Territorial Statehouse State Historic Monument, in Fillmore, is a red sandstone building that dates from the early 1850s. Once the capitol of Utah Territory, it is now a museum dedicated to territorial history.

The spectacular rock formations of Fisher Towers, north of Moab

Other Interesting Places to Visit:

Beehive House, in Salt Lake City, the restored 1854 home of Brigham Young, has been restored and is open to the public. Nearby *Lion House* once contained Brigham Young's offices.

Bonneville Salt Flats, 125 miles (201 kilometers) west of Salt Lake City, is a perfectly flat salt bed that is the site of the world's fastest automobile speedway.

Drive Through the Ages Geological Area, north of Vernal, crosses the Uinta Mountains. Interpretive signs describe rock layers that date back a billion years.

Fisher Towers, north of Moab, 1,500-foot- (457-meter-) high rock formations, and nearby *Castle Tower* have been made famous by movies and television commercials. Nearby is the *Priests and Nuns Formation.*

Great Salt Lake, 17 miles (27 kilometers) west of Salt Lake City, is the second saltiest body of water in the world (after the Dead Sea).

Moki Dugway Overlook, a few miles north of Mexican Hat, offers a spectacular panoramic view of the *Valley of the Gods,* the *Goosenecks of the San Juan River, Monument Valley,* and the *Four Corners* area.

Mormon Temple, in St. George, erected in 1877, was Utah's first completed Mormon temple. Nearby is the *Brigham Young Winter Home.*

State Capitol, in Salt Lake City, was completed in 1914. This copper-domed building was modeled after the United States Capitol in Washington, D.C.

Temple Square, in Salt Lake City, is a 10-acre (4-hectare) landscaped park that contains the *Mormon Temple,* built between 1853 and 1893; the *Salt Lake Tabernacle,* home of the famed Mormon Tabernacle Choir; the historic *Visitors' Center;* and many monuments.

This is the Place Monument, in Salt Lake City's Pioneer State Park, was erected in 1947 to commemorate the hundredth anniversary of the arrival of the first Mormons in the Salt Lake Valley.

Trolley Square, in Salt Lake City, is a multilevel complex of specialty shops, restaurants, theaters, and night spots.

IMPORTANT DATES

10,000 B.C.?-A.D. 400?—Desert Culture people inhabit the Great Basin

400?-1300?—Fremont and Anasazi people begin farming in Utah

1300?—Shoshonean-speaking tribes enter Utah; Navajos enter 100-200 years later

1540—Captain Garcia Lopez de Cardenas may have entered Utah

1776—Friars Silvestre Vélez de Escalante and Francisco Atanasio Domínguez explore Utah

1824—General William Henry Ashley's fur trappers cross South Pass and enter Utah; Jim Bridger discovers the Great Salt Lake

1826—Ashley holds the first annual *rendezvous* in Utah for fur trappers and traders

1827—Jedediah Strong Smith passes through Utah on the first American overland journey to California

1830—*The Book of Mormon* is published; Church of Jesus Christ of Latter-day Saints is organized at Fayette, New York

1832—Antoine Robidoux establishes a post in the Uinta Basin

1841—The Bartleson-Bidwell party crosses Utah on the way to California

1843—Captain John Frémont explores the Great Salt Lake Region

1844—Joseph and Hyrum Smith are shot to death by a mob at Carthage, Illinois; Brigham Young and the Quorum of Twelve Apostles head the Mormon church

1845—Miles Goodyear builds a permanent post near Ogden

1846—The Donner-Reed emigrant party crosses Utah

1847—The first Mormons arrive in Utah, begin irrigation, and lay out Salt Lake City; Brigham Young is named president of the Mormon church

1848—Sea gulls supposedly save the Mormon pioneers' crop from crickets; Utah becomes part of the United States when the Treaty of Guadalupe Hidalgo ends the war with Mexico

1849—Brigham Young is named governor of the Provisional State of Deseret; discovery of gold in California brings thousands through Utah; a Perpetual Emigrating Fund Company is organized to aid poor converts traveling to Utah

1850—Congress creates the Territory of Utah to replace the State of Deseret and names Brigham Young the first territorial governor; the *Deseret News* begins publication; the University of Deseret (later renamed the University of Utah) is established; Utah's population numbers 11,380 in the first territorial census

1851—Salt Lake City, Ogden, and Provo are chartered; Fillmore is named the territorial capital

1852—Plural marriage (polygamy) is publicly proclaimed as a Mormon doctrine

1853—Construction begins on the Mormon Temple in Salt Lake City; the Walker War (Ute) begins; Captain John W. Gunnison is killed in a battle with Indians

1856—Handcart migration begins, bringing many new people to Utah

1857—The Utah War begins when President Buchanan appoints Alfred Cumming territorial governor, replacing Brigham Young, and sends federal troops to put down Mormon "rebellion"; a party of travelers passing through Utah is slaughtered in what becomes known as the Mountain Meadows Massacre

1859—Colonel Thomas Kane helps negotiate the end of the Utah War

1860—The Pony Express begins a year and a half of operations through Utah

1861—Nevada Territory is created from western Utah; Colorado Territory is created from part of eastern Utah; telegraph lines meet in Salt Lake City, connecting the Atlantic and Pacific coasts

The Mormon Tabernacle, shown here under construction, was completed in 1867.

1862 — Congress passes an antipolygamy law; the Salt Lake Theater opens

1863 — Colonel Patrick Connor defeats a band of Shoshones at the Battle of Bear River; the first mining claim in Utah is filed by George Ogilvie

1864 — Congress creates the Uintah Reservation for Ute Indians

1865 — The first non-Mormon church is established by Congregationalists; Ute-Black Hawk War begins

1867 — The Mormon Tabernacle is completed in Salt Lake City

1868 — Zion's Cooperative Mercantile Institution (ZCMI) begins operations; the creation of Wyoming Territory reduces Utah to its present-day dimensions

1869 — The Union Pacific and Central Pacific railroads meet in Golden Spike ceremony at Promontory Summit, completing the first transcontinental railroad in the United States; Major John Powell explores the Green and Colorado rivers

1872 — Smelting and refining begin in the Salt Lake Valley

1874 — The United Order (a communal social and economic system) is organized among Utah Mormons

1875 — Brigham Young Academy (later Brigham Young University) is founded

1876 — John D. Lee is convicted and executed for his participation in the Mountain Meadows Massacre

1877—Brigham Young dies in Salt Lake City; the St. George Mormon Temple is completed

1882—Congress passes the Edmunds Act, taking the vote away from those who practice, or believe in, polygamy

1883—The Denver and Rio Grande Western Railroad connects Denver with Salt Lake City

1887—Congress passes the Edmunds-Tucker Act in its war on polygamy

1888—Utah State Agricultural College (later Utah State University) is established

1890—Mormon authorities prohibit new polygamous marriages; free public schools are established

1893—President Benjamin Harrison extends amnesty to polygamists; the Mormon Temple in Salt Lake City is dedicated

1895—Utah's present constitution is adopted at the seventh constitutional convention

1896—President Grover Cleveland proclaims Utah as the forty-fifth state; the first state legislature convenes; Martha Hughes Cannon becomes the nation's first woman to be elected a state senator

1897—Utah's first national forest, the Uinta, is established

1899—Alice Merrill Horne sponsors a bill to create an annual state art exhibit and to establish a state art collection

1900—An explosion in an underground mine at Scofield kills two hundred

1903—Reed Smoot is elected to the United States Senate and an effort—ultimately unsuccessful—begins to deny him his seat

1905—Open-pit mining of low-grade copper ore begins at Bingham Canyon

1907—Oil is produced from the fields around the Virgin River

1913—The Strawberry Reservoir Project, the state's first large water-diversion project, is completed, bringing water to the Great Basin

1914—The state capitol in Salt Lake City is completed

1915—Labor organizer Joe Hill is executed for the murder of a Salt Lake City grocer and his son; his trial and execution attract worldwide attention

1917—Simon Bamberger is elected the state's first non-Mormon governor

**Weeping Rock, in
Zion National Park**

1918 — Emma Lucy Gates Bowen opens a grand opera company in Salt Lake City

1919 — Congress establishes Zion National Park

1923 — Prehistoric Indian remains at Hovenweep are declared a national monument

1927 — An explosion at the Castle Gate coal mine kills 127 workers

1928 — Congress establishes Bryce Canyon National Park

1933 — Cedar Breaks National Monument is established

1934 — Official automobile racing begins at Bonneville Salt Flats

1937 — Capitol Reef National Monument is established

1940 — The Utah State Symphony Orchestra is founded

1942 — American Citizens of Japanese ancestry are interned in Millard County under executive order of President Roosevelt

1947—Maurice Abravanel becomes music director of the Utah Symphony

1948—J. Bracken Lee, an archconservative, is elected to the first of his two terms in office as governor; Bernard De Voto receives the Pulitzer Prize in history for his book *Across the Wide Missouri*

1952—Uranium is discovered near Moab

1964—The Flaming Gorge Dam on the Green River is completed; Congress establishes Canyonlands National Park; construction of the Glen Canyon Dam in Arizona backs up the Colorado River and floods miles of Utah's most scenic canyons

1967—Construction begins on the Central Utah Project, designed to bring water to Central Utah; state laws address the problem of air pollution

1968—SOCIO (Spanish Speaking Organization for Community, Integrity, and Opportunity) is established; six thousand sheep in western Utah are poisoned by nerve gas being tested by the United States Army at Dugway Proving Ground

1969—Salt Palace convention center opens in Salt Lake City

1971—Capitol Reef National Monument becomes Capitol Reef National Park

1978—Black men are admitted to the Mormon priesthood; Arches National Monument becomes Arches National Park

1982—Barney Clark, a retired dentist, becomes the recipient of the nation's first artificial heart transplant at the University of Utah medical center

1985—United States Senator Jake Garn becomes the first senator to make a spaceflight while still in office; Mark Hoffman is involved in pipe-bomb murders as part of a plot to defraud the Mormon church

1987—The Salt Lake City Trappers set a professional baseball record by winning twenty-nine consecutive games—the longest winning streak in the history of organized baseball

1988—Polygamist Addam Swapp battles Utah police in Marion; after a $400-million rehabilitation, the world's largest open-pit copper mine reopens at Bingham Canyon

1989—Scientists at the University of Utah claim to have achieved cold nuclear fusion, an announcement that engenders worldwide controversy

IMPORTANT PEOPLE

Maurice Abravanel (1903-   ), symphonic conductor; as
conductor and music director of the Utah Symphony (1947-80),
built it into one of the nation's top orchestras and in the process
greatly enhanced the artistic life and climate of the Salt Lake area;
his many recordings in the 1960s and 1970s brought the orchestra
international acclaim

Maude Adams (1872-1953), born in Salt Lake City; actress; best
remembered for her performance in the title role of Sir James M.
Barrie's *Peter Pan* (1905-07); her other successful roles included
leads in such plays as *The Little Minister* (1897-98), *Quality Street*
(1902), and *What Every Woman Knows* (1908-09)

MAUDE ADAMS

Daniel (Danny) Ainge (1959-   ), professional athlete; all-
American basketball and baseball player at Brigham Young
University; played baseball for the American League Toronto Blue
Jays; joined the National Basketball Association Boston Celtics in
1982; starting guard on two world-championship teams; member
of the NBA All-Star team (1988)

Hal Ashby (1936-1988), born in Ogden; motion-picture director
and producer; among his more popular films are *Shampoo* (1975)
and *Coming Home* (1978)

DANNY AINGE

James Pierson (Jim) Beckwourth (1798-1867), explorer and
mountain man; Utah fur trapper with the Ashley company who
lived with the Crow Indians for six years and learned their ways;
his memoirs were published as *The Life and Adventures of James P.
Beckwourth* (1856)

Ezra Taft Benson (1899-   ), public official and Mormon church
leader; U.S. secretary of agriculture (1953-61); head of the
Council of Twelve Apostles of the Church of Jesus Christ of
Latter-day Saints (1973-75); president of the church (1985-   )

Reva Beck Bosone (1895-   ), lawyer, judge, politician; the only
woman from Utah ever elected to the U.S. House of
Representatives (1949-52)

EZRA TAFT BENSON

James (Jim) Bridger (1804-1881), explorer, trapper, and scout;
sometimes called the "Daniel Boone of the Rockies" because of his
many explorations in the area; considered the first white man to
explore the Great Salt Lake (1825); served as a guide on the
1832-35 expedition of Captain Benjamin Bonneville

Faun M. Brodie (1915-1982), college professor, author; her
prizewinning biography of Joseph Smith, *No Man Knows My
History*, was the first scholarly study of Smith

Juanita Brooks (1898-   ), historian, author; her most important
works are *Mountain Meadows Massacre* and a biography of John D.
Lee

JIM BRIDGER

GEORGE Q. CANNON

BUTCH CASSIDY

GEORGE H. DERN

PHILO T. FARNSWORTH

John Moses Browning (1855-1926), born in Provo; gunsmith and inventor; along with his brothers Matthew and Jonathan Edmund, invented the Winchester repeating rifle, the Colt automatic pistol, and the Browning automatic rifle

Nolan Kay Bushnell (1915-   ), born in Ogden; computer programmer and executive; created the first coin-operated video game (1971); chairman of Atari Corporation (1972)

Jerry Hatten Buss (1933-   ), born in Salt Lake City; real estate executive and sports club owner; owner of the Los Angeles Lakers (National Basketball Association) and the Los Angeles Kings (National Hockey League) franchises

George Quayle Cannon (1827-1901), Mormon pioneer and leader; arrived in Salt Lake City in 1847; served as private secretary to Brigham Young, chancellor of the University of Deseret (later the University of Utah), and editor of the *Deseret News*; as a territorial delegate to Congress, he worked hard for Utah's admission to statehood

Butch Cassidy (1887-1912), born George Leroy Parker in Circleville; noted outlaw who used the Utah maze country in the Colorado Plateau as a hideout; his life story was the basis of the movie *Butch Cassidy and the Sundance Kid*

Patrick Edward Connor (1820-1891), military officer and anti-Mormon leader; commanded the Utah Military District; encouraged mining as a way of attracting non-Mormons to Utah; after resigning from the army, he became a leader of the anti-Mormon Liberal Party

Reverend France A. Davis (1946-   ), influential civic leader and minister of Salt Lake City's Calvary Baptist Church

Bernard Augustine De Voto (1897-1955), born in Ogden; editor, literary critic, and historian of the American West; his major works include *Mark Twain's America* (1932), *The Year of Decision: 1846* (1943), the Pulitzer Prizewinning *Across the Wide Missouri* (1947), and *The Course of Empire* (1952)

George H. Dern (1872-1936), mine owner and politician; Utah governor (1925-33) who championed progressive legislation and Utah's first income tax; U.S. secretary of war (1933-36)

Marriner Stoddard Eccles (1890-1977), born in Logan; banker, economist, government official; chairman of the Board of Governors of the Federal Reserve System (1936-48); U.S. representative to the Breton Woods International Monetary Conference (1948)

Philo Taylor Farnsworth (1906-1971), born in Beaver; inventor, electronics and television pioneer; as a fifteen-year-old high-school student, he worked out the basic concepts of television; gave the first display of television at the Franklin Institute (1934); later held more than 165 radio and television patents

John Charles Frémont (1813-1890), explorer, surveyor, and public official; famous for his explorations of much of the area between the Rocky Mountains and the Pacific Ocean; explored the Great Salt Lake area (1842-43) and was the first to name it the "Great Basin"

Gene Fullmer (1934-), born in West Jordan; boxer; middleweight boxing champion of the world (1957, 1959-62)

Edwin Jacob (Jake) Garn (1932-), born in Richfield; insurance executive, naval pilot, and politician; mayor of Salt Lake City (1972-74); U.S. senator (1974-); current ranking Republican on the Housing and Urban Affairs Committee and member of the Senate Appropriations Committee; a retired brigadier general in the Utah Air National Guard; he won national fame in 1985 when he flew aboard the space shuttle *Discovery*, orbiting the earth 109 times

Otto Abels Harbach (1873-1963), born in Salt Lake City; Broadway producer and librettist; wrote the lyrics for about fifty musical comedies including *Roberta* (1933)

Orrin Grant Hatch (1934-), lawyer, politician; U.S. senator (1977-); a staunch conservative, a strong supporter of President Reagan during the 1980s; ranking Republican on the Labor and Human Resources Committee and member of the Senate Judiciary Committee

William Dudley "Big Bill" Haywood (1869-1928), born in Salt Lake City; miner and labor leader; started working as a miner at the age of fifteen; led the Western Federation of Miners (1900-05) and helped found the International Workers of the World (IWW), sometimes called "Wobblies" (1905); convicted of sedition in 1918 for opposing the U.S. war effort in World War I; escaped to the Soviet Union where he spent the remainder of his life; one of two Americans buried in the Kremlin

Grant Johannesen (1921-), born in Salt Lake City; musician; first prizewinner of the Ostend (Belgium) International Competition (1949); since then has given concerts with major symphony orchestras of the world

David M. Kennedy (1905-), born in Randolph; banker and government official; secretary of the treasury (1969-71); ambassador to NATO (1971-75)

Helen Kurumada (1917-), community leader and civil-rights activist; the first director of the Utah State Office of Asian Affairs (1983-)

Esther R. Landa (1912-), civil-rights and women's activist; president, National Council of Jewish Women (1975-79); first director of University of Utah Women's Studies Program; president, National Committee on Employment for the Handicapped; Board of Governors, Hebrew University, Jerusalem; cofounder, Project Headstart in Utah

JOHN CHARLES FRÉMONT

JAKE GARN

OTTO HARBACH

ORRIN G. HATCH

129

JOHN W. MARRIOTT

MERLIN OLSEN

JOHN WESLEY POWELL

IVY BAKER PRIEST

John Willard Marriott (1900-   ), born in Marriott; restaurant and hotel executive; founded the Marriott Hotel and Restaurant chain, which became one of the nation's largest hotel chains

James (Jim) McMahon (1959-   ), professional football player; all-American quarterback at Brigham Young University, where he set fifty-six college football records for passing; led the Chicago Bears to the National Football League Super Bowl Championship (1985)

Peter Skene Ogden (1794-1854), Canadian fur trapper; one of the first trappers to enter the Salt Lake area, where he was highly regarded by Indians and trappers alike

Merlin Jay Olsen (1940-   ), born in Logan; athlete, actor, and sports announcer; all-American lineman at Utah State University, from which he graduated Phi Beta Kappa (1962); played for the Los Angeles Rams of the National Football League (1962-76); played in the Pro Bowl a record fourteen consecutive years; became a sportscaster, acted in the television series "Little House on the Prairie," and starred in the series "Father Murphy"

Donald Clark (Donny) Osmond (1958-   ) and **Marie Olive Osmond** (1959-   ), born in Ogden; singers, actors, entertainers; costars of the "Donny and Marie" television series (1976-79); have appeared in many television specials, have recorded many hit albums, and appeared in the Donny and Marie film *Going Coconuts*

Helen Zeese Papanikolas (1918-   ), born in Carbon County; historian, author; her study of the history of ethnic groups in Utah, particularly Greeks, made it clear that Utah history is much more than the study of the Mormon church and the Mormon people; author of *Toil and Rage in a New Land*, *Immigrants in Utah*, and *The Peoples of Utah*

Esther E. Peterson (1906-   ), born in Provo; consumer advocate and government official; assistant secretary of labor (1961-69); special assistant to President Carter for consumer affairs (1977-80); received the Presidential Medal of Freedom (1981)

John Wesley Powell (1834-1902), military officer and government explorer; after losing an arm at the Battle of Shiloh, he led the first exploration of the Green and Colorado rivers; his *Exploration of the Colorado River of the West and Its Tributaries* (1869) helped make him famous; Lake Powell is named in his honor

Ivy Baker Priest (1905-1975), born in Kimberly; banker and government official; treasurer of the United States under President Dwight D. Eisenhower

Merlo John Pusey (1902-   ), born in Woodruff; author and editor; won the 1952 Bancroft Medal and the 1952 Pulitzer Prize in biography for *Charles Evans Hughes* (1951)

George Wilcken Romney (1907-   ), politician, businessman; born of Mormon parents in a church colony in Mexico; grew up in Salt Lake City; general manager of the American Automobile Association; president of American Motors; governor of Michigan (1963-69); U.S. secretary of housing and urban development (HUD) (1969-72)

GEORGE ROMNEY

Karen Shepherd (1941-   ), women's-rights advocate, journalist, and teacher; in the mid-1970s, founded, edited, and published *Network* magazine, still the most important journal in Utah that addresses women's issues

Jedediah Strong Smith (1799-1831), explorer, fur trapper; entered the Salt Lake area as early as 1825 and became the first white man to travel the length of Utah from north to south and west to east

Joseph Smith (1805-1844), religious leader and founder of the Church of Jesus Christ of Latter-day Saints; died before his followers reached Utah

Reed Smoot (1862-1941), born in Salt Lake City; Mormon leader and politician; elected to the U.S. Senate in 1903, but did not actually gain his seat until 1907 because of opposition to Mormon practices; became a leader of conservative Senate Republicans; opposed U.S. membership in the League of Nations; best known as the cosponsor of the Hawley-Smoot Tariff Act of 1930, which raised U.S. tariffs to an all-time high, setting off worldwide tariff wars that added to the severity of the Great Depression of the 1930s

REED SMOOT

Eliza Roxey Snow (1804-1887), poet; pioneer author of many poems, at least a dozen of which have become popular Mormon hymns

Wallace Stegner (1909-   ), writer and educator; attended the University of Utah, where he later taught; wrote *The Gathering of Zion* (1964), a story of the Mormon Trail, and *The Big Candy Mountain* (1943); received the 1972 Pulitzer Prize in fiction for *Angle of Repose* (1971)

GEORGE SUTHERLAND

George Sutherland (1862-1942), jurist, politician; U.S. senator from Utah (1905-22); associate justice of the U.S. Supreme Court (1922-38); best remembered for his conservative views and opposition to much of President Franklin D. Roosevelt's New Deal legislation

May Swenson (1919-   ), born in Logan; poet, author, and teacher; won the 1981 Bollingen Prize in Poetry (Yale University) and many other awards; her works include *A Case of Spines* (1958), *To Mix With Time* (1963), and *Half Sun Half Sleep* (1967)

MAY SWENSON

Walkara (1808?-1855), born in a village on the Spanish Fork River near Utah Lake; Ute Indian Chief known as Walker, perhaps the best known and most powerful Indian leader in the Great Basin region from about 1830 until his death

BRIGHAM YOUNG

LORETTA YOUNG

STEVEN YOUNG

Wilford Woodruff (1807-1898), Mormon leader; was among the advance party that accompanied Brigham Young to Utah in 1847; president of the Mormon church (1889-98); best known for the 1890 Woodruff Manifesto, which called for the end of plural marriage in the Mormon church

Brigham Young (1801-1877), Mormon leader and territorial governor; joined the Mormon church in 1832 and served as missionary and as member of the church's Council of Twelve Apostles; succeeded Joseph Smith as leader of the church and directed the Mormon exodus (1846-47) from Nauvoo, Illinois, to the Great Basin, where he chose the site for Salt Lake City; directed the settlement of more than 350 cities and towns; is recognized today as a master of organization and planning and as an inspired religious leader

Loretta Young (1914-   ), born in Salt Lake City; motion-picture actress; made nearly one hundred Hollywood films during the 1930s and 1940s; won the 1947 Academy Award as best actress for her starring role in *The Farmer's Daughter*; hosted "Loretta Young Presents," a weekly television anthology (1953-60)

Mahonri Young (1877-1957), born in Salt Lake City; sculptor; grandson of Brigham Young; studied art at New York City's Art Students League; favored themes dealing with workers or prizefighters, but is best known for his *Sea Gull* and *This is the Place* monuments

Steven Young (1961-   ), born in Salt Lake City; professional football player; set new records for passing at Brigham Young University; quarterback for the San Francisco 49ers of the National Football League

GOVERNORS

Heber M. Wells	1896-1905	J. Bracken Lee	1949-1957
John C. Cutler	1905-1909	George D. Clyde	1957-1965
William Spry	1909-1917	Calvin L. Rampton	1965-1977
Simon Bamberger	1917-1921	Scott M. Matheson	1977-1985
Charles R. Mabey	1921-1925	Norman H. Bangerter	1985-
George H. Dern	1925-1933		
Henry H. Blood	1933-1941		
Herbert B. Maw	1941-1949		

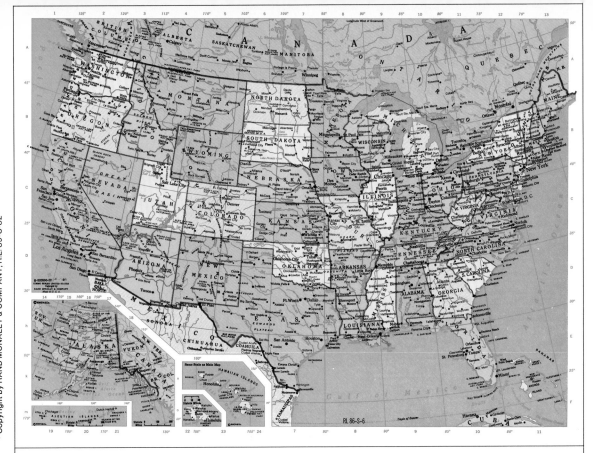

Topography

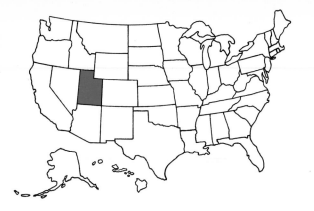

MAP KEY

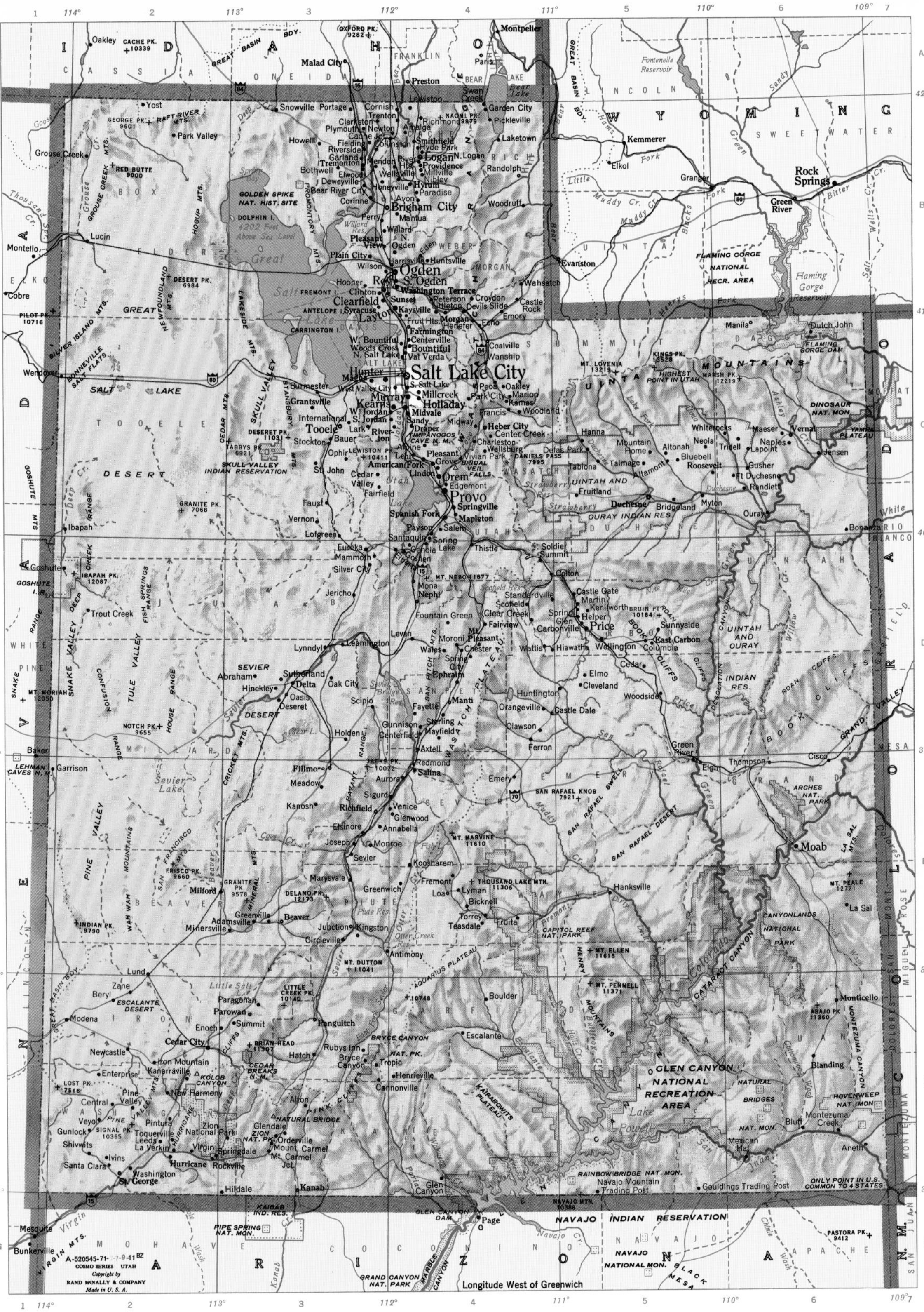

IDAHO

WYOMING

UTAH

COLORADO

ARIZONA

NEVADA

Salt Lake City

Ogden

Provo

Great Salt Lake

GREAT SALT LAKE DESERT

UINTA MOUNTAINS

Moab

St. George

Cedar City

GLEN CANYON NATIONAL RECREATION AREA

NAVAJO INDIAN RESERVATION

Longitude West of Greenwich

COSMO SERIES UTAH
A-520545-71   -7-9-11 B2
Copyright by
RAND McNALLY & COMPANY
Made in U.S.A.

Lambert Conformal Conic Projection

HOGS

BEEF CATTLE

SHEEP

POULTRY

POTATOES

VEGETABLES

FRUIT

SUGAR BEETS

WHEAT

BARLEY

ALFALFA

MANUFACTURING

DAIRY PRODUCTS

OIL

NATURAL GAS

MINING

SALT

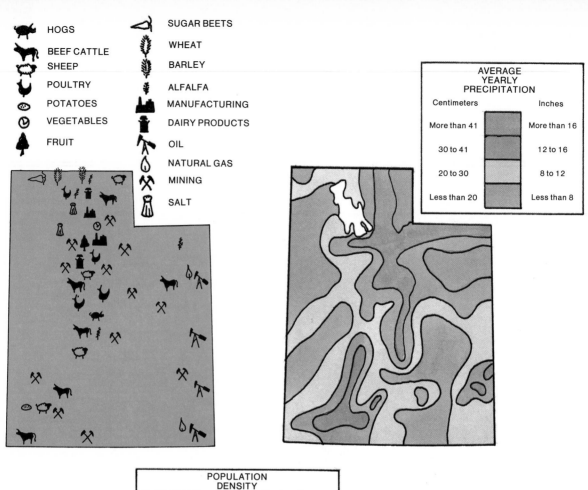

AVERAGE YEARLY PRECIPITATION

Centimeters		Inches
More than 41		More than 16
30 to 41		12 to 16
20 to 30		8 to 12
Less than 20		Less than 8

POPULATION DENSITY

Number of persons per square kilometer		Number of persons per square mile
more than 40		more than 100
4 to 40		10 to 100
2 to 4		5 to 10
Less than 2		Less than 5

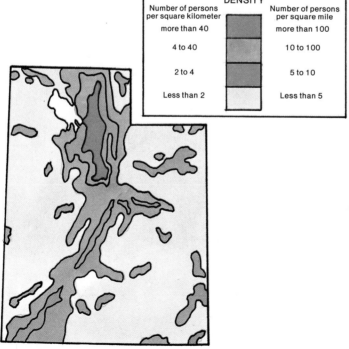

MAJOR HIGHWAYS

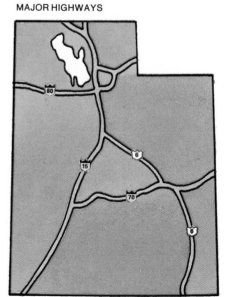

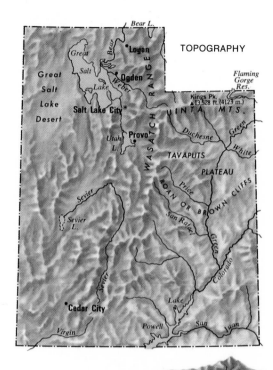

TOPOGRAPHY

Below Sea Level | 100 m. 328 ft. | 200 m. 656 ft. | 500 m. 1,640 ft. | 1,000 m. 3,281 ft. | 2,000 m. 6,562 ft. | 5,000 m. 16,404 ft.

Courtesy of Hammond, Incorporated

Maplewood, New Jersey

COUNTIES

Blazing aspen trees along Duck Creek in Dixie National Forest

INDEX

Page numbers that appear in boldface type indicate illustrations.

Coral Pink Sand Dunes State Park

Picture Identifications

Front Cover: Bryce Canyon
Back Cover: Mormon Temple, Salt Lake City
Pages 2-3: Rainbow over a Monument Valley rock formation
Page 6: Fall color at Logan Canyon
Pages 8-9: Mirror Lake, Uinta Mountains
Page 18: Montage of Utahans
Page 24: Anasazi Indian cliff dwellings in southern Utah
Pages 36-37: W.H. Jackson's painting *Handcart Pioneers, 1857*
Page 51: Church of Jesus Christ of Latter-day Saints Office Building, Salt Lake City
Pages 64-65: The Capitol, Salt Lake City
Pages 74-75: Skiing at Snowbird
Pages 86-87: Jenson Living Historical Farm, an authentic 1917 Mormon pioneer farm near Logan
Page 108: Montage showing the state flag, state tree (blue spruce), state bird (sea gull), state insect (honeybee), state flower (sego lily), and state animal (elk)

About the Author

Betty McCarthy was born and grew up in Chicago. She received a degree in Chinese history from the University of Chicago, and did graduate studies in Far Eastern and modern history at the same institution. Before turning to new interests, she worked for a number of years training teachers and developing the curriculum for the social-studies division of a major correspondence high school.

She now lives in Chicago with her husband, their cat and dog, and hundreds of indoor and garden plants. Her interests include horticulture, writing, and traveling to the Rocky Mountain states of the United States and the Andes Mountain regions of Peru and Ecuador.

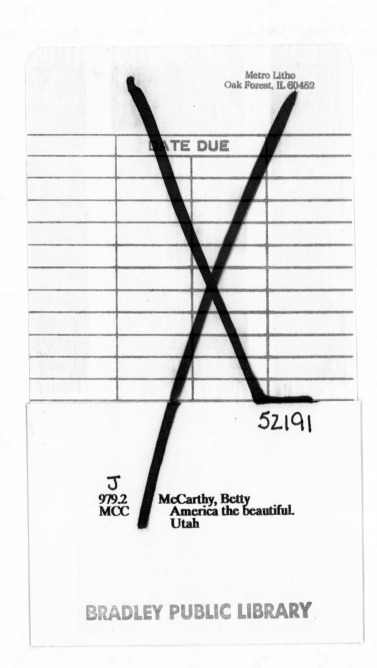